SUCCESS
HABITS

SUCCESS HABITS

PROVEN PRINCIPLES for GREATER
WEALTH, HEALTH, and HAPPINESS

———————

NAPOLEON HILL

St. Martin's Essentials ⚐ New York

www.stmartins.com

Designed by Devan Norman

The Library of Congress Cataloging-in-Publication Data is available upon request.

ISBN 978-1-250-30807-8 (trade paperback)
ISBN 978-1-250-30808-5 (ebook)

Our books may be purchased in bulk for promotional, educational, or business use. Please contact your local bookseller or the Macmillan Corporate and Premium Sales Department at 1-800-221-7945, extension 5442, or by email at MacmillanSpecialMarkets@macmillan.com.

First Edition: December 2018

10 9 8 7 6 5 4 3 2 1

CONTENTS

FOREWORD

A young magazine reporter from the mountains of southwest Virginia, Napoleon Hill was assigned to interview American steel magnate Andrew Carnegie. Mr. Carnegie was impressed with young Napoleon's intelligence and ambition, and at the end of the three-day interview Mr. Carnegie asked him if he would devote twenty years of his life, without pay, to researching and writing the first book ever on the philosophy of success developed and applied by America's leaders. With some trepidation but little hesitation, Napoleon said yes and assured Mr. Carnegie he would not only begin the project but he would complete it.

Complete it he did, and twenty years after that 1908 interview, Napoleon Hill published his first book, titled *Law of Success*. It was followed in 1937 by what became the best-selling success book of all time, *Think and Grow Rich*. Napoleon went on to publish many more motivational books and lectured extensively throughout the United States in succeeding decades. He was enjoying semi-retirement in the 1950s, in his late-sixties, when Chicago insurance tycoon W. Clement Stone urged the by then "Dr." Hill to present a number of radio and television lecture programs. Always desirous of teaching his success principles to new audiences, he accepted and put on several such programs throughout America.

Dr. Hill and his wife established the Napoleon Hill Foundation in 1962, intending that it would continue to teach his principles after he was gone. He died in 1970, and the Foundation they established continues to carry on to this day, spreading his principles throughout the world in scores of languages. I have been a trustee of the Foundation since 1997, and its executive director since 2000.

A few years ago I came across the dusty tapes and transcripts of several of Dr. Hill's radio and television lecture programs that had been tucked away in the Foundation's archives. They had never been published. Foundation trustees were thrilled to have the opportunity to resurrect them, and thus was born the Napoleon Hill Is on the Air series of books. The book you are holding is one in that series, a transcription of weekly radio programs presented in 1952 in Paris, Missouri.

How did Napoleon Hill come to give a series of radio interviews in the small town of Paris, Missouri? The answer illustrates one of his seventeen principles of success developed in his twenty years of research: the principle is that every adversity carries with it the seed of an equivalent advantage. Dr. Hill had put on a seminar in St. Louis, Missouri, a large city on the Mississippi River, which had turned out to be unprofitable. More money was spent promoting it than was received in attendance fees. However, a longtime follower of Dr. Hill, Bill Robinson, a businessman in Paris, Missouri, was in the audience, and was inspired to invite Dr. Hill to put on a series of lectures in Paris.

Paris at that time was a town of only 1,400 people. It is located in rural northeastern Missouri, on the central fork of the Salt River, far from any major metropolitan areas. St. Louis, the nearest large city, is approximately 135 miles away. Young people were leaving Paris for greater employment opportunities in bigger cities. Robinson was worried about the decline of the town, and arranged to have nearly 100 townspeople attend the series of lectures over several weeks. They would be broadcast on local radio, and Dr. Hill would receive $10,000. There were skeptics in Paris who thought the lectures would be little more than a medicine show, but Dr. Hill soon won them over with his powerful messages.

Following these inspirational broadcasts, many Paris citizens banded together in discussion groups. A local minister presented a series of sermons based upon Dr. Hill's teachings. A number of new businesses, as many as ten by one account, sprouted in this small town as a direct result of the lectures. A year after the broadcasts, Dr. Hill said that an elderly Paris resident told him that "nothing had come to that community within the past fifty years which had made such a profound impression on so many of the people as had been made by the teaching of my philosophy."

A movie titled *A New Sound in Paris* was made, documenting the changes that were brought about in that small community by Dr. Hill's lectures. It was seen by hundreds of thousands of people and helped to spread the success principles taught by Dr. Hill. Unfortunately, it appears to have been lost to history.

Napoleon Hill loved Paris. It was wholesome small-town America. Mark Twain had been born nearby, in Florida, Missouri, and his books reflected the Midwestern culture of honesty, determination, and hard work. Beloved American artist Norman Rockwell painted a famous picture of the bustling local newspaper office in

Paris in 1946 that appeared in the *Saturday Evening Post*. The wandering Salt River, with its three forks, beautified the area and ultimately poured into the Mighty Mississippi. One fork passed under one of the few covered bridges ever built in Missouri.

Napoleon Hill once said, "The path of least resistance makes all rivers, and some men, crooked." That phrase aptly describes the meandering Salt River. Fortunately, thanks in some part to Napoleon Hill's efforts, it does not describe the men and women of Paris, who worked hard to avoid that path and to make their lives, the lives of their families, and their community successful and happy.

As you read this book, the first and only publication of these radio lectures, you will encounter some men who followed the path of least resistance, but Dr. Hill will show you the way to reject this path by the application of his principles of success.

The lectures concentrated on a few of the seventeen success principles, ones that Dr. Hill believed would be especially helpful to the people of Paris. The first two dealt with Definiteness of Purpose, viewed by many Hill followers as the most important of the laws of success. The next two focused on the importance of Accurate Thinking. The next two explained how Applied Faith was necessary to the attainment of success. The next two dealt with the Causes of Failure and how to overcome them with persistence and decisiveness. The ninth showed how Self-Discipline was essential to success. The next two dealt with the importance of a Pleasing Personality to achieving success. The final two dealt with Cosmic Habit Force, the only one of the seventeen principles of success that Dr. Hill claimed had not been recognized by anyone before he discovered it.

In the lectures on Definiteness of Purpose, Dr. Hill explained how the laws of nature reflect a definite purpose and plan. He detailed the nine basic motives that propel people to carry out their plans and accomplish their purposes. In the Accurate Thinking lectures, Dr. Hill explained the difference between inductive and deductive reasoning and showed how to separate important facts from the unimportant. He detailed how people should challenge the opinions and statements of others by asking the simple question "How do you know?" Falsehoods, he said, came with warning notes. He listed the enemies of accurate thinking, perhaps most importantly the emotions, concluding that "Accurate thinking is cold-blooded thinking."

In his lecture on Applied Faith, Dr. Hill explained how to develop it using one's definite major purpose, mastermind alliances, and the principle of learning from adversity. He provided many examples of industrialists and inventors who used Applied Faith to benefit mankind.

Changing his approach, the next two programs dealt with the causes of failure. He listed the major causes and gave concrete examples of how to overcome them through persistence and decisiveness. He hoped to convince his listeners, many of whom were down on their luck, that they did not have to surrender to these causes of failure. In his Self-Discipline lecture, Dr. Hill told of thirteen challenges in his own life that were overcome by Self-Discipline. In an especially eloquent manner he described the importance of using Self-Discipline to budget and control one's use of time.

Dr. Hill listed twenty-five major factors contributing to a Pleasing Personality, and invited his listeners to take inventory and grade themselves against these factors. He admitted that he himself did not always live up to these standards. He gave examples of those who did, and also listed fifteen things one should not do if one wanted to have a Pleasing Personality.

The final two lectures were on Cosmic Habit Force and explained how Dr. Hill discovered this concept upon reading *Think and Grow Rich* for the first time a year and a half after he wrote it. Cosmic Habit Force is the law by which one acquires habits to carry out one's major purpose. Dr. Hill provides a number of ways one can use this principle to accomplish one's goals and objectives.

I believe you will find these timeless radio programs to be informative and that they will show you the way to achieve success and happiness. It was Dr. Hill's intention to teach and inspire the people of Paris to use his principles to overcome adversity, to avoid the path of least resistance, to get on the straight and narrow, and to work hard to turn their lives around. I know that it worked for Paris, and I am confident that it can work for you as well.

—Don Green,
Executive Director, Napoleon Hill Foundation

SUCCESS HABITS

1

DEFINITENESS OF PURPOSE

Good evening, ladies and gentlemen. Tonight we are starting our series of radio programs here in Paris, Missouri, in which I will explain the principles of success I have learned and developed over more than forty years. I am delighted to be in your city and hope you will benefit from what I have to tell you.

The first principle I will speak about is definiteness of purpose. Definiteness of purpose doesn't sound like a very imposing or a very dramatic subject, but ladies and gentlemen, it's the beginning of all achievement worthy of mention. Wherever you find anybody who is succeeding, you'll find a person who has adopted the principle of definiteness of purpose in connection with the things he does, and he follows that principle at all times. That is why I have given it first position in these broadcasts, and why I will discuss it in our second broadcast as well.

I'm going to give you an illustration of the importance of being absolutely definite in connection with your major purpose. Some years ago, right after the end of World War Number One, I went into my safe-deposit box and took out my written definite major purpose, and in the paragraph in which I had stated my projected income for that year, 1919, it read "$10,000 per year," I took my pencil and added a zero to those figures, making the number "$100,000," and laid the written statement back in the vault. I believed I needed to set my sights higher! And I don't think it was more than three weeks before a man from Texas came into my office and made me an offer of $100,000 a year if I would go down to Texas and spend three weeks out of each month writing sales literature for him. I accepted that contract, which he drew up, signed it, and went down there and ultimately raised some $10 million for him.

He had drawn up a contract that was, I would say, very tricky. It specified that unless I stayed an entire year I wouldn't receive any of my salary. In a little while, I began to see that he was misusing these funds, and instead of staying the entire year, I turned him in to the FBI and went back to Chicago, and lost my entire salary up to that time. Then I went into my vault again and took out my definite major purpose, which I had written down, and read it carefully. Here is the way it read: "I will earn during the year 1919 the sum of $100,000."

I saw immediately, when I read it carefully, what was wrong with that statement, and I wonder if you could tell me what's wrong with it before I tell you. There's no doubt in the world but that I did earn the $100,000, because there's hardly anyone who wouldn't be glad to pay $100,000 for services which raised capital in the amount of $10 million. I earned it, all right, but I didn't get it. I want to tell you now why I didn't get it.

I didn't get it because I left two important words out of my affirmation. Go over the statement as I have given it to you, and see if you can supply those two important words. I'll repeat the statement again: "I will earn during the year 1919 the sum of $100,000." Now, isn't that definite, or isn't it? You think that's definite? It sounds definite in a way, doesn't it? No, there were two words left out. I should have said, "I will earn AND RECEIVE $100,000 during the year 1919."

Do you think if I had written it that way that it would have made any difference in the makeup of this crooked man who, perhaps from the very beginning, intended to cheat me? Do you think it would have made any difference as to the money I would have received? I'll tell you that it would have made a difference, and I want to tell you why. If I had placed emphasis on the fact that I was going to receive that money after I earned it, I would have taken that contract, which he drew up, to my attorney, and we would have gone over it very carefully, and my attorney would have provided a paragraph in there whereby I would get that money from month to month as I earned it. That's the difference it would have made.

The majority of people who go into contracts and various and sundry arrangements and relationships with other people do so with such indefiniteness that there seldom is what the lawyer would call a meeting of the minds. One person will understand one thing, and another person will understand something entirely different.

We need contracts because, unfortunately, some people are cheaters who cannot be trusted, or they will take the easy way rather than the honorable way. Taking the path of least resistance makes all rivers and some men crooked, and that was certainly the case with this man from Texas.

I want to give you another illustration about the importance of definiteness of purpose. Some fourteen years ago Bill Robinson, from here in Paris, purchased a copy of my book *Think and Grow Rich*. He read it and was impressed by it, and as he was reading it, he said to himself, "Some of these days I'm going to meet this man Hill. I'll get him to come over here to Paris, and he's going to deliver a talk for our people."

Now, "some of these days," ladies and gentlemen, is not definite. Fourteen years passed. He was lying in bed, reading one of the St. Louis papers in which he saw an advertisement of mine, indicating that I was conducting a course in St. Louis. This time he made another statement. He jumped out of bed and said, "I'm going over to St. Louis and see that man, and I'm going to have him over here immediately." That was approaching definiteness. He did come over there, and here I am.

He could have done that fourteen years ago, if he had said when he read that book, "I like this message, I like that author; I'm going to have him over here within a month." If he had put a definite time upon his intentions, you may be sure that I would have been over here a long time ago.

Definiteness of purpose. I have noticed that men who are successful, like Mr. Andrew Carnegie, Henry J. Kaiser, Henry Ford, and Thomas A. Edison, all move with definiteness of purpose. Generally, any great leader, when he tells one of his subordinates to do something, he not only tells him what to do, but he tells him when to do it, he tells him where to do it, he tells him why he should do it, and importantly, he tells him how to do it, and then more important than all of these, he sees to it that the man does what he tells him. He doesn't take no for an answer.

That's what constitutes a great leader, a man who knows precisely what he wants and who can pass that information on to people who are subordinate to him in terms that they can understand and that will impress them.

During the war, Mr. Kaiser was engaged in a great variety of war work, manufacturing military items which the government needed badly. In order to ensure that the necessary raw materials would be at his plant when he needed them, when, for example, he would order a carload of a certain type of steel, he didn't just send an order down to the United States Steel Corporation to ship him a carload of a certain kind of steel. He said that he wanted that steel at his plant on a certain date, and then he sent a couple of expediters over to the steel plant to ride that car through, with instructions that if any railroad man dared to set that car off on the siding for any purpose whatsoever, those expediters were to stop him from doing it, and to keep that car moving, or else not come back. Their jobs wouldn't last any longer.

That was pretty definite, too. As a result, Mr. Kaiser made a world-famous record in the business of building ships. He never had built ships before, but he did understand the principle of definiteness. Incidentally, if you know anything about Mr. Kaiser, you know that that's one of his outstanding qualifications today. It's one of the reasons why he has been a successful man. He has known what he wanted to do, he's laid out a plan for doing it, and he's been very definite about all of his plans.

This "what to do, when to do it, where to do it, why to do it, and how to do it" is what I call my WWWWH formula. It wouldn't be a bad idea for each of you in the audience to have a nice pin made up for your lapel or your dress with a WWWWH on it. Most people who see that pin won't know what it means, but you will. It will keep in your mind the fact that when you tell a person to do something, you must be definite about it. You must tell him what to do, when to do it, where to do it, why to do it, how to do it, and then you must get after him and see that he does it.

I'm talking to you now about the difference between a successful man and an unsuccessful man. You take an unsuccessful person and generally, when he gives instructions or expresses his desires, he does it in a very slipshod, loose, indefinite manner, and as the results come back they are just like that, too.

When I was commissioned by Andrew Carnegie some forty-four years ago to become the author of the world's first practical philosophy of individual achievement, I was kept at Mr. Carnegie's house for three days and nights. He was studying me carefully, and I didn't know that I was under observation at all. I didn't know the purpose of it. I found out years later that what he wanted to find out about me more than everything else was if I had this quality of being definite about things that I undertook to do.

At the end of the third day, he called me into his library and he said: "We've been talking here for three days about a philosophy which I think the world needs, a philosophy that will give the man in the streets the know-how gained by successful men like myself who got that knowledge by a lifetime of experience through the trial-and-error method. I want a philosophy in simple terms that will give the man of the streets the benefit of all that has been learned by successful men. I want to ask you a question about that."

Then he put this question to me. He said, "If I commission you to become the author of this philosophy, introduce you to the outstanding men of this country who will collaborate with you, the men who are authorities on the subject of success, are you willing to devote twenty years of your life to research, earning your own living as you go along, without any subsidy from me? Yes or no?" I fidgeted around for several seconds, I suppose. It seemed to me like an hour. Finally, Mr. Carnegie said, "Well," and he started to ask me another question. I broke in. I said, "Yes, Mr. Carnegie, I not only will accept your commission, sir, but you may depend upon it that I will complete it." He said, "That's what I wanted to hear you say." He also said, "I wanted to see the expression on your face when you said it, and I wanted to hear the tone of voice in which you said it."

He made up his mind then and there to give me a commission that had been denied to other men, some of them college professors. He said that when he put that question to them, their reaction time in answering ran all the way from three hours to three years, and some of them never did give an answer. He wanted somebody who could be definite, who could make up his mind when he had all of the facts at hand, whether he would do a thing or whether he wouldn't.

When I started the *Golden Rule Magazine,* beginning on Armistice Day 1918, I didn't have any capital with which to do it. I'd been in the service of the president of the United States throughout that war. The school of which I was the president and owner had entirely disintegrated as the result of the war. But I wanted to publish a *Golden Rule Magazine.* I'd had that in mind for a great number of years. The time had come, I believed, when the public would welcome a magazine of that sort.

All I needed was a little matter of $100,000 to start with. That was all. If I'd gone into a bank to borrow

$100,000, the chances are that they would have pressed a button secretly, and a couple of big plug-uglies would have pounced on me and turned me over to the police, because they would have thought I was out of my mind.

I couldn't have borrowed $100,000 from private sources, because what I had to offer as security was intangible. So I worked out a plan for getting that money, or the equivalent of it, and it took me only three days to have it in hand. Before I approached the man that I intended to give the privilege of lending me this $100,000, I sat down to my typewriter and I wrote the leading editorial that I intended to publish in the front of that magazine, just as if I had the money already in hand. I closed the editorial by saying that "I will need at least $100,000 to get this magazine started. Where the money is coming from, I don't know, but one thing I do know, and that is that I shall publish and distribute the *Golden Rule Magazine* this year." That was very definite.

I took the editorial to a very wealthy printer, Mr. George B. Williams of Chicago. I allowed him to invite me to the Athletic Club of Chicago for lunch. I allowed him to spend $3.85 for a lunch which I didn't eat, didn't even touch. Meantime, I was talking, telling him about this magazine, and when I thought that I had told him all that he needed to know, I pulled out this editorial and handed it to him. When he read that last quotation, that

I do not know where the money's coming from, here is what he said. He said: "I like your idea, I like you. I have liked you for a long time, and I think you can do the job. You bring your copy in, I'll print the magazine, we'll put it on the newsstands and we'll sell it, and when it's sold, I'll take my money first and if there's anything left, you can have it."

That, ladies and gentlemen, was the way that the *Golden Rule Magazine* was started, and it attained a circulation of over 500,000 the first six months, and it cleared a net profit above all expenses the first year of $3,150.

Later on, when I was writing editorials for Bernard McFadden's magazine, I told him about this, and he said: "Hill, I've known you a long time, and I have great respect for your ability, but there's something wrong with your figures. You must not have been good in mathematics when you went to school, because I happen to know that in order to start a national magazine with any degree of assurance that you'll make it go, you have to have at least a million dollars, and the chances even then are about fifty-fifty that you'll get none of it back."

Well, it scared me to death after I found out that I had done something that couldn't be done. It's a good thing that I didn't know that before I started. There are so many people, ladies and gentlemen, that never undertake things that they would like to do because they are afraid they can't carry them through. Or they're waiting for all of the circumstances to be just right before they start.

Do you know that if you wait for all circumstances to be just right before you undertake something that you've been planning, maybe for a great number of years, you'll never start, because circumstances never are just right. If you want to do a thing badly enough, get together all of the information you can about it, provide yourself with all of the equipment that is available, and start where you stand to do what you can about it at that time. The chances are, as strange as it may seem, as you use the tools that you have at hand, whatever they may be, that other and better tools will sometimes miraculously be placed at your service.

I wonder if you members of my radio audience wouldn't be interested in knowing what my definiteness of purpose is for the next five years. Would you be interested in that? I'm going to tell you about it, because you're going to have the opportunity of seeing me in action. You're going to hear this announcement. You're going to watch, step by step, how I go about carrying it out.

I am going to work full-time again, ending my recent life of leisure, and resume writing books and lecturing. There's several reasons why I am going to do this. In the first place, personally, I have as much money as I need, if

I didn't get any more the rest of my life. I have enough to see us through, according to our style of living. All excess funds are going to be used exclusively in promoting the distribution of this philosophy throughout the world. I want the philosophy published in every one of the leading languages on earth, and I'm going to see to it that that's done.

I have found out something as the result of my coming to towns like Paris that I didn't know before about this philosophy, and it's given me new hope and new courage. It's given me a new slant on definiteness of purpose, and that is that the people at the grass roots of the population, in little towns like this, are ready and hungry for this philosophy to come into their lives. Because, after all, this is a philosophy of individual economy. It's designed to help the individual to balance his financial affairs. It's a sound philosophy because it's been tested by the keenest brains in the world. And it is a philosophy dealing with individual finances and material things.

We're living in an age of frustration, an age of fear, an age of anxiety. It would be almost impossible to go through an audience like this and find a person who didn't have some sort of personal problem that he doesn't know how to solve for the moment. This success philosophy is intended to solve individual problems. Whether you realize it or not, each and every one of you who listens to these broadcasts will be spreading sunshine, spreading joy, and spreading courage. You will have more confidence, and you will give more confidence to those you come into contact with. You will have definiteness of purpose, too, and as a starting point you will have a purpose to improve yourselves.

Ladies and gentlemen, our time is up for tonight. Join me next time for further discussion of this most important principle, definiteness of purpose.

2

MASTERING YOUR DEFINITE PURPOSE

Welcome back, ladies and gentlemen. Tonight I will discuss how important this principle of definiteness of purpose is, and how you can apply it to achieve success.

Ladies and gentlemen, you may be interested in knowing why I am so positive in connection with my statements about this principle and about all the principles I will discuss in upcoming broadcasts. I want you to know that each and every one of these principles that you will be studying here has been checked and double-checked by the laws of nature.

When you can get confirmation of the soundness of a principle by going to nature herself, you're not going to go wrong. I want to give you an idea of the extent and the scope to which nature goes in making use of this lesson that we're dealing with tonight, definiteness of purpose. Our greatest demonstration of the universal application of the principle of definiteness of purpose may be seen by observing how nature applies it.

First of all, it is seen in the orderliness of the universe, and the interrelation of all of the natural laws. Isn't it a marvelous thing to know that this small ball of mud on which we live, revolving around the sun entirely every 365 days, keeping its proper distance from all of the other planets and from the sun, isn't it a marvelous thing to know that all of it is organized? When the sun goes down in the evening, we go to sleep knowing that it's going to arise again in the east next morning. So far as I've been able to understand and hear, the sun never has failed to come up after it went down in the evening. I have known of many cloudy times when you couldn't see it here in Missouri, but it was there, just the same.

The orderliness of things goes to prove beyond any question of a doubt that there is a first principle or cause back of it all and that nature is very definite in carrying out that plan. How many billions or trillions or quadrillions of years this old planet has been floating around according to a definite plan, nobody knows. But we do know there's something definite about it, and nature doesn't allow that definiteness to be interfered with by any force whatsoever.

Yes, and we see the definiteness of nature in the fixation of all of the stars and planets, and their immovable relationship to one another. That relationship is so definite, ladies and gentlemen, that the astronomers can figure and foretell hundreds of years in advance the approximate relationship of any two given stars or planets at a given time. You couldn't do that if there wasn't a definite plan of operation being carried on by nature.

And then you see it in the operation of the law of gravitation, without cessation anywhere for any purpose whatsoever. Have you ever heard of the law of gravitation being stopped, or anyone violating it without ill effects? It's there, it's definite, it never varies in any form whatsoever. You can adjust yourself to it, and it becomes very helpful. But if you don't adjust yourself to it, it can become very destructive.

You see it in the overall balancing of life on this earth, so that no single species may dominate. Do you know that the human race wouldn't last twelve months if nature didn't have a definite plan for balancing the insects and the birds, and the great variety of things smaller in importance than human beings? Sometimes she sends an epidemic of grasshoppers that do a great deal of damage, but in a little while, a flock of birds, gulls or something else, come over and gorge themselves on those grasshoppers to keep that balance going properly.

Some time ago, some people brought some starlings over here, I believe from England, with the intention of destroying some insect that the starlings like to feed on. But nature didn't like that unbalancing of her affairs, and so she multiplied those starlings very rapidly, and they now have become a nuisance. I could put an adjective in front of that word "nuisance" if I wanted to. When you start interfering with nature's overall balancing of things, you get into trouble, because she has a definite plan of keeping everything in balance, according to her overall intentions. This ought to be a cue to human beings.

Then you see it in the process of evolution, through which the operation of everything in existence, whether animate or inanimate, is the outgrowth of something of the same nature which preceded it. Isn't that an interesting thing? Did you ever hear of a farmer planting wheat and going out and being surprised to know that corn had come up instead of wheat? No, you never did. Nature has a definite way of causing everything that reproduces itself to reproduce something very closely akin to its ancestors. That applies to human beings, the same as everything else. Nature doesn't vary in her definiteness in carrying out these laws.

And it is seen in the impossibility of creating or destroying either matter or energy, or the modification of the amount of either. Isn't it an astounding thing to recognize that you can't destroy energy or matter? You can't decrease or increase the amount of either. You can transform them from one state to another, but you cannot interfere with the amount. When you use up a certain amount of energy, nature has a way of replenishing it and balancing her storehouse of it. She doesn't allow you to run out of the use of electricity, for instance. Someone said to me some time ago, "Well, some of these days, all of this electricity'll be used up, and then what's going to happen?" That would be a catastrophe, wouldn't it? Ladies and gentlemen, don't worry; that's not going to happen.

Nature has everything throughout the universe balanced, and her plans are set, her laws are fixed. She doesn't change her mind and decide one day that she'll have the sun come up, and the next day that she'll not have it come up. She doesn't get careless and allow our earth to come into contact with some other planet and cause a smash-up.

Almost every year we see some excitement in the newspapers about a group of misguided and unfortunate people who predict the ending of the world. Generally they dispense with all of their worldly goods, let other people cheat them out of them, get up on top of houses and in trees, and get ready for the ascension to, well, wherever it is they're going. Because the world's coming to an end. I've seen that happen, I think, six times during my lifetime, and this old world is rolling right along, just like it was the first time I ever observed it. I suspect it'll be rolling along in the same way for a long time to come.

If you want to get a good idea of the importance of definiteness, you should watch nature in everything she does, and you'll get some very fine ideas. You should also observe the profoundly ingenious system of the human mind, which has been so definitely fixed through its design that every individual may project himself into circumstances of the life of his own choice. He may fix the space he shall occupy as an individual, and determine in many respects his own earthly destiny, this being the only thing over which any individual has complete control.

Isn't it a marvelous thing to know that nature has definitely given to every human being the right to determine his own earthly destiny, to use his mind, to engage in the sort of activities he wants to engage in? Right away you're going to say, "Well, that doesn't apply to Russia today, and it didn't apply to Germany for a time. And as matters are going right now, if we keep on, it's not going to apply to us here in the United States. We're not going to be so free to do whatever we want to, work when we please, engage in the occupation we please."

But, ladies and gentlemen, let me turn you backwards some five or six thousand years and call your attention to the fact that every single solitary person who has ever undertaken to divert the plans of nature has come to grief. Those men over in the Kremlin and in other parts of the world who are now trying to take away from mankind this great prerogative of control of the individual mind are going to come to grief. There's the element of timing there; sometimes we think the timing is strung out too much. Right now, it seems that it is. But if I'm not misinformed, nature has a great deal of time on her hands. She can wait quite a long while to punish Joseph Stalin and the others, but punish him she will. That's definite. She will never allow him to take away the liberty of the people, because that's the one thing that the Creator saw to it that every human being should have: definiteness and the impossibility of circumventing or suspending even for one second any of nature's laws.

Now, surely, there is fixation definiteness of purpose. You've never heard of anybody circumventing any of nature's laws, or undertaking to do it, without coming to grief . . . sometimes immediately. You can try to defy the law of gravitation, sure. You can get on top of a tall building and jump off, if you're foolish enough to do it. Unless you have somebody intervening down there with a net or something to catch you in, you'll come to a lot of grief, but you won't know anything about it.

Sure, you can try to defy nature's laws. You can defy all of them. But if you do, you're going to have to pay a price. Nature has definite penalties for the violation of all of her laws, and definite rewards for the observation of them. There's no escape from that. It wouldn't make any difference what your religion is, not the slightest difference. You would have to come to the conclusion that nature has definite plans for dealing with human beings here on earth now, and that she has great rewards to give out to individuals who find out what her plans are and adapt themselves to those plans, and great penalties for those who fail to do so.

It's one of the burdens, and one of the privileges, of this success philosophy I have discovered to guide people in a practical, understandable way to the ways of nature, to the laws of nature, and to the ways and means of adapting the individual's actions in life to those laws.

Now, ladies and gentlemen, I want to give you some of the important factors that go into the business of applying definiteness of purpose. The first one is that the starting point of all individual achievements is the adoption of a definite purpose accompanied by a definite plan for its attainment followed by appropriate action. There's three key words in there to remember, if you can't remember all I've said. There must be a purpose, there must be a plan, and there must be an action—purpose, plan, action. It's not enough to say, "Well, some of these days, I'm going into the lumber business." Some of these days. Some of these days never come. But if you said, "Starting next week, I am going to order a stock of material and go into the lumber business in Paris, Missouri," and if you have the capital available for doing it and start out doing it, that's definite.

The second factor is that all individual achievements are the results of a motive or a combination of motives. Everything you do from the time you reach the age of consciousness of yourself until you die is the result of a motive. Nobody ever does anything without a motive. And there are only nine basic motives.

The importance of what I want to do now is to impress you that these nine basic motives are the ABC's of success. You should never, under any circumstances, ask or expect anybody to do anything without planting in that person's mind a motive or a combination of motives justifying what you ask them to do. Under no circumstances would I ever ask anybody to do anything until I first felt in my own heart that I had planted in that person's mind a motive, and also had justified the request. If you'll do that, you'll never go wrong.

Here are the nine basic motives, some combination of which is used by all people who accomplish anything:

The first one is the emotion of love. You'd be surprised to know how many human relationships are established, how many fortunes are made and how many fortunes are lost, and how many things happen in this world as a result of this motive of love. It is the greatest of all of the motives and the greatest of all of the emotions, and yet the most dangerous, especially for those who let loose of both ends of the string and say, "I'm going off the deep end." I have known of people doing just that.

The second of these nine basic motives is the emotion of sex, that great creative force that is employed by nature to perpetuate the species of all living things.

Third is the desire for material wealth. That's sort of an inborn trait. It's one of the outstanding motives that inspire men to engage in great undertakings. I've never heard of anybody who turned down an opportunity to make money legitimately. And sometimes, unfortunately, they're willing to make it otherwise.

The fourth of these nine basic motives is the desire for self-preservation. That's an inborn motive. You do things that at times seem almost superhuman as a result of carrying out this motive for self-preservation. Many have been the times since I've been driving an automobile during the last forty-odd years that I've performed feats of driving that I couldn't begin to perform deliberately, if I had plenty of time. That is to say, these are cases of near emergencies when something inside of me would take over the wheel and throw the car off of the road, and then back on it again. I had something happen like that the second time that I came up here to Paris. My car turned around entirely in the road, turned around and started back up toward Paris. I think the car wanted me to come back up here and finish the job. There I was, headed this way again. The desire for self-preservation is an outstanding motive.

The fifth basic motive is the desire for freedom of body and mind. The Creator not only gave you the right to freedom, the inborn right to control your own mind and by that control to gain freedom for yourself, but he planted in your mind a desire for that freedom. If there is one thing that we here in America prize above all other things today, it's our privilege of being ourselves, saying the things we want to say, doing the things we want to do. Of course, we can't always say the things we'd like to say, but we can come pretty close to it. Freedom. We have a great amount of freedom in the United States, more than they have in any other nation on earth. That's one of our motives for doing some of the things we do now, in order to protect that freedom.

The sixth motive is the desire for personal expression and recognition—personal expression and recognition. I've never known of anybody yet that didn't want to do one or the other of two things: first, be able to make a speech— What about? Oh, anything—and second, to write a book— What about? Oh, anything. The desire for personal expression is an inherent desire, and one of the great motives that prompt men and women to engage in far-reaching undertakings.

Perhaps it was the motive of desire for personal expression that prompted me to go through twenty years of near starvation while I was organizing this philosophy and getting it ready for the public. I don't think any other motive could have caused me to have kept at that job when it wasn't profitable.

The seventh major motive is the desire for perpetuation of life after death—that's also an inherent motive.

Now I come to the last two motives, and they're both negative. Number eight is the desire for revenge. You would be surprised at the amount of energy spent by people every day as the result of their attempt to take revenge on somebody for some real or imaginary grievance. The desire for revenge is a very destructive thing. It may work hardship or injustice upon others, but it's sure to work hardship on the one who engages in it. There are lots of people in this world of whom I don't approve, some that I don't particularly like. But if I had every privilege in the world of engaging in any form of revenge, I wouldn't do it. Not because there aren't some people that deserve it, perhaps, but because I couldn't afford to hurt myself. If you're living the proper way, have a well-balanced life, you get to the point at which you don't want to take revenge on anybody for anything.

The ninth and last motive is the grandfather of them all, ladies and gentlemen, the emotion of fear.

You'll not be a free agent as long as you're afraid of anything, or anybody. You've got to become free in your own mind. If there's something that you fear, find out why you fear it and get rid of that fear. If it's something that you can do something about, do it, and if it's something you can't do anything about, forget about it. Or at least fill your mind so full of something else that you won't be thinking about it and nursing it.

The next factor that enters into this business of definiteness of purpose is this great, outstanding truth: namely that any dominating idea, plan, or purpose which you hold in your mind through repetition of thought is taken over by the subconscious section of the mind and acted upon through whatever natural and logical means that may be available. You will observe that, through my tone of voice, I emphasized certain words in that statement. Through whatever *natural* and *logical* means that may be available. I didn't say anything about supernatural means. I don't know anything about working through supernatural means. I only know about working through natural laws.

I want each and every one of you to feel that there is a part for you to play. There is some person or persons or group of people with whom you have contact to whom you may start teaching this philosophy. You may not be the best teacher in the world, but make that your definite purpose, that you're going to commence expounding the philosophy and passing it on to other people who may need it. You'll find that as you undertake to teach others, as you begin to tell them about it, you will begin to get a better grip on the philosophy yourself. That's a law of nature, too: whatever you do to or for another person, you do to or for yourself. You'll never, ladies and gentlemen, get the full benefit of this philosophy until you look around you and find somebody who needs it, and start teaching that person. Let him become acquainted with us, let him tune in on this atmosphere and make up his own mind whether this fellow Hill came up here to take in a lot of people and get them all stirred up, as one man said that he thought I did. Well, I'll admit, just in case there's any doubt about it, I did come up here with the intention of getting a lot of people stirred up, awakened, if you please, and interested in doing something not only to help themselves, but to help this community in which they live.

Thank you for joining me tonight, friends. Please tune in next time when I will explain the importance of accurate thinking in reaching your success goals.

3

ACCURATE THINKING

Hello, friends. Tonight we begin discussion of the subject of accurate thinking. There are a lot of people in this world who believe that they think accurately, but the majority of them don't think at all; they just think that they think. Accurate thinking involves certain factors, which I'm going to explain to you. They're not complicated, but I want to warn you in advance that if you wish to become an accurate thinker instead of a snap judgment thinker, you have to have a technique, you have to follow a system, and you have to stick to that system.

First of all, there are three important fundamentals in the business of accurate thinking, and here they are: number one is the principle of inductive reasoning based on the assumption of unknown facts or hypotheses. "Inductive reasoning" means that you do not have all of the facts, but you assume that certain facts must exist. For example, if you are going to think accurately on the subject of God, whether or not there is a God, you've never met him, you've never seen him, you never have met anybody who has met him or seen him, and yet your reasoning on the subject would have to be of the inductive nature. When you begin to look around at the marvelous organized factors in the universe, and in this little world in which we live, you would be forced to the conclusion that there is such a power as that which many call God, whether you call it by that name or some other. That would be inductive reasoning.

Number two, there is deductive reasoning based upon known facts—facts that you know to be true—or what are believed to be facts. There are a lot of people who stumble on that one, because they assume to have facts when all they are dealing with is hearsay evidence or gossip; something that "they" said, or "something that I read in the papers." When someone starts to tell me something, and prefaces his remarks by saying "I see by the papers," I reach up, figuratively speaking, and pull down my mental earmuffs and refuse to let anything he says register in my mind. Because having been a newspaperman once upon a time, and having known a great many newspapermen, I do know that newspapers often make mistakes. They're not always accurate.

The third factor that enters into the business of accurate thinking is logic—that is to say, guidance by past experiences, similar to those under consideration at a given time. Logic. Ladies and gentlemen, if you will take the average circumstance where you're trying to do some accurate thinking, and after you have reached your decision in connection with it, or perhaps before you have reached your decision, if you will submit the whole proposition to the principle of logic, to see whether it's logical that the opinion or decision you're about to arrive at is correct or not, you'll save yourself an awful lot of trouble.

Those are the three factors that go into the business of accurate thinking.

There are two major steps that you must take in accurate thinking, and here they are. Two steps only. First, you must separate facts, or what you believe to be facts, from fiction or hearsay evidence. That's the first thing you do. When you're dealing with any subject whereby you're going to reach a decision in connection with your thinking, you must immediately search all of the factors that enter into that and see whether they constitute facts or fiction or hearsay evidence. That's step number one. As I go along analyzing this subject, ladies and gentlemen, it would be very beneficial to you if you would compare these rules that I am giving you with your own method of thinking, and see wherein you fall short, if at all. It might be a good idea for you to analyze some of the people you know best by these rules, to see how many of them are doing accurate thinking.

First, you separate fact from fiction or hearsay evidence. Then, after you've done that and you know what the facts are, or believe that you know, you've made that separation, you've thrown out the hearsay evidence, you're dealing only with those things that you can prove, you separate those facts into two classes, and one is called "important" and the other "unimportant."

Would you know how to go about distinguishing the difference between an important fact and an unimportant fact? How many of you would be able to make that differentiation? Show me by your hands. What? Don't you know the difference between an important fact and an unimportant fact? Or are you just overly modest? An important fact, ladies and gentlemen, may be assumed to be any fact that can be used by you to an advantage in the attainment of your major purpose, or any of your minor desires leading toward the attainment of your major purpose. That to you is an important fact, and all other facts are relatively unimportant, and most of them are out and out worthless, so far as you're concerned.

I could mention to you a hundred facts of things that have happened since I left my home in St. Louis this morning and drove up here to Paris, but I'll say ninety-nine percent of them wouldn't be of any importance one way or the other. There's only one fact in connection with my trip up here that is important, and that is that I arrived here at this studio on time, and that I'm now fulfilling my scheduled lecture.

Now you know what an important fact is. If you will watch yourself in connection with your actions throughout the day, you will be amazed at the number of unimportant facts that take up a lot of your time, facts which, no matter how you handle them or how you relate yourself to them, mean nothing to you except a waste of time. If you're going to be successful people in the upper brackets of success, if you're going to learn to think accurately and use that knowledge to lift you high in the strata of success, then you have got to learn not only to separate important facts from unimportant facts, but you've got to form a habit of devoting most of your time to important facts—that is to say, facts that will bring you some definite, discernible benefit leading toward the object of your major purpose in life, or the attainment of some of your minor purposes.

Oh, if you're going to follow that rule, there'll be a number of bridge parties that you'll have to cut out. There'll be a number of things that you indulge in that you might just as well discontinue, because you're only wasting time, and you're not dealing with important facts at all.

Next, I want to call your attention to the business of

having opinions. Opinions usually are without value, because they are typically based on bias, prejudice, intolerance, guesswork, or hearsay evidence. Most people have opinions about any and every subject that you might imagine, and the majority of those opinions are not worth anything at all because they are not arrived at by practical or scientific means. Two men some time ago were discussing the merits of Dr. Einstein's theory of relativity. One of them said, "Do you really believe in Dr. Einstein's theory of relativity?" And the other man said, "Heck, no. What does that man know about politics, anyway?" He thought the theory of relativity was a system of politics, yet he had an opinion on it.

It would be interesting to you, and perhaps beneficial, my friends, if you would study yourself carefully every time in the future that you are getting ready to express an opinion about anything. Examine yourself carefully to see how you came by the influences and circumstances that enabled you to express that opinion, to see whether they came from sound sources, from hearsay evidence, or from something that you read or something you heard from unreliable sources. Opinions. No opinion is safe unless based upon known facts, or at least what are believed to be facts, after you have exhausted all the possibilities of searching for facts. No one should express an opinion at any time about anything without a reasonable assurance that it is founded upon facts.

Had you ever thought of that, that you shouldn't express an opinion on any subject at all unless it is based upon either known facts or what you believe to be facts? Had you ever stopped to think about it, that the vast majority of your opinions are based upon something far different from facts or known facts? You haven't made the effort to gain the facts, but you have an opinion nevertheless. You have no right to that opinion, because there's nothing on which to found it.

Someone asked me not long ago what my opinion of the Korean War situation was. I said, "Well, that's a question that can't be answered in one sentence. I have a lot of opinions about it. I have a lot of opinions about the people who started it. I have a lot of opinions about the way it's being conducted." I couldn't answer with one opinion; I would have several opinions, and all of them based upon what I have seen happen since that war started. That is, they were based upon facts.

Advice, too, is often worth little or no attention. Free advice, volunteered by friends and acquaintances, usually is not worthy of consideration. Someone has said that anything in the world that you get for nothing is worth exactly the price you pay for it, and that is particularly true of free advice. It makes no difference what you want to do, what your plans are, where you're going or what you're doing, what your aims in life may be. The moment you begin to talk about them, you'll find a lot of people around you with a lot of free advice, and particularly those closely related to you.

When I started to organize the world's first philosophy of individual achievement, it's true that eventually I had some five hundred of the most outstanding men of America who gave freely from their experiences in order to help me complete this philosophy. But all of those five hundred combined were nothing in comparison with the free advice that I got from my immediate family. Here I was, doing twenty years of research with the most intelligent brains in the world helping me out, and still, two or three members of my family thought they could tell me more about what I was doing, more about its weaknesses, than could all of those five hundred men combined. And the advice was free. Of course, I didn't have to take it. Of course, I didn't take it. If I had taken it, I wouldn't be here tonight, talking to you about this business of accurate thinking. I had to learn to go on my own, to do some thinking of my own.

Accurate thinking and accurate thinkers permit no one to do their thinking for them. If you're going to be an accurate thinker in the strict sense of that term, you have got to get into the habit of becoming responsible for your own thinking and your own opinions and your own ideas. It's all right to seek information from other people; get all the knowledge you can, get all the facts you can. But in the final analysis, don't let anybody make up your mind for you about anything. Is that clear enough, or shall I state it over? Pretty clear, isn't it? Don't let anybody make up your mind for you about anything. Reserve unto yourself the last word in your thinking. If you let others think for you, you are taking the path of least resistance, like those rivers I mentioned in a previous broadcast, and meandering without self-control, taking a crooked path.

Don't be silly enough, though, to think that you can do accurate thinking without some help from the outside. Many times, you'll have to have a lot of outside help. That's why we have the mastermind principle. Mr. Edison was the most important and the most successful inventor the world has ever known. His inventions were based upon thinking. But before he could think accurately, he had to have the scientific knowledge and brains and education of men who helped him do his thinking, who supplied the facts. He put those facts together in new combinations.

It's all right for you to seek information, but when you get that information, you must submit it to the law of logic. You must submit it to the law of evidence, and make sure that when you make a decision, the facts that you have accepted are real facts, and not merely hearsay evidence. Hearsay evidence is secondhand evidence you cannot get to the bottom of, and it is inherently unreliable.

If you follow literally what I am suggesting to you, you can see readily that you're going to have to rearrange some of your habits. Matter of fact, you have to rearrange radically some of your habits of thinking. You'll have to read your newspaper a little bit more carefully, you'll have to read it with a question mark in your mind; you'll have to question the things that you read, you'll have to quit this business of being influenced by what the gossiping neighbors say, and do a lot more thinking on your own. It's not safe to form opinions based upon newspaper reports. "I see by the papers" is a prefatory remark usually branding the speaker as a snap-judgment thinker. "I see by the papers," or "I hear tell," or "They say." When anybody starts off volunteering information supposed to be facts based upon those prefatory remarks, just close up your ears and pay no attention unless you have some supporting evidence, and you'll get along very much better in your thinking than you have been doing in the past.

Scandal-mongers and gossipers are not reliable sources from which to procure facts on any subject. Scandal-mongers, gossipers. Did you ever hear of any—of course, you don't have any here in your town, but in some communities they do have them. I meet them in almost every community I go to, and among all facets of people, except my own audience. Of course, they're above and beyond the business of passing on scandal and gossiping, small talk.

Oh, there's a lot of fun in gossiping. I hear some gossip oftentimes that I get a great kick out of, especially when it's about myself. Then I know more about the subject than the person doing the gossiping. But that doesn't make any difference; the gossipers will talk. But if you're going to be scared off of your line of duty, or off of your activities, or off of your plan or purpose in life by what the gossipers say, ladies and gentlemen, you might as well not start anything, because you won't get anywhere.

A long time ago there was a man who passed this way, a very gentle soul who came to the world for the purpose of seeing if he could do something to soften the nature of mankind and make men live together a little bit more peacefully. He didn't get along so very well in the face of these gossipers and scandal-mongers and small-talk people. They didn't all accept him. They killed him. But the spirit of Jesus survived and changed the world in immeasurable ways.

You'll not be accepted the moment your head sticks up above the crowd in any sort of undertaking. The gossipers will begin to take you apart, take you down to size, if you let them do it. But if you're an accurate thinker, you'll pay no attention to what is said about you. You'll pay more attention to seeing that the unkind things said about you are not true, and that's your entire responsibility if you're an accurate thinker. Beyond that, you'll pay no attention to what people say.

Wishes are often fathers to facts—did you know that? Had you ever thought about that? I wonder if you've ever been guilty of fathering facts through wishes. Hopeful wishing, they call it sometimes. Most people have a bad habit of assuming facts to harmonize with their desires. One of the easiest things to do upon the face of this earth is to assume facts to fit the nature of what you want to do. Wishes can only be converted to facts by taking action, not merely assuming.

I once had the experience of interviewing over an extended period of time the late gangster Al Capone. I was astounded to know that, far from him having been a criminal, offending the law and the people of this country, he believed he was a very much maligned man. He claimed Uncle Sam's long nose had been stuck into a legitimate business that he was conducting—he said it was legitimate. He said that by selling whiskey during prohibition he was merely selling a thirst quencher to people who were thirsty. They were paying for it, they were glad to have it, and Uncle Sam should have kept his nose out of his legitimate business. He had sold himself that idea: He had convinced himself that he was being very much maligned by the law.

I have never yet met a person, a criminal, a person breaking the law, that hadn't sold himself the idea that he was well within the law, well within his rights, and the law had no reason or right to touch him. It's one of the easiest things in the world to justify what you're doing in life, and if you don't watch yourself, you'll justify yourself beyond the point of reason if you're not an accurate thinker.

Information is abundant, and most of it is free, but facts have an elusive nature, and generally there is a price attached to them. Somebody asked me not long ago why I didn't just go about the country teaching this philosophy free of charge, not charging anything for it, if I didn't need to make any money. Do you know what I said to that person? I said, "Do you belong to a church?" He said, "Why, yes, sure I do." I said, "Do you go to church?" and he said, "Yes, sometimes." I said, "Is your church always filled on Sunday morning?" "Oh, no, oh, no," he said, "very few of the seats are filled." And I said, "Do you know what's wrong with the churches?" He said, "No, I don't know whether there's anything wrong with them or not." I said, "Have you ever attended one of my lectures?" He said, "Yes, I attended all of your lectures here up to the present time." This man, by the way, lives in this community. I said, "Did you notice that on the opening night of our radio broadcasts in Paris, Missouri, one of the worst nights of the winter, that people came from as far away as sixty-five miles? They showed up, they were all there, the room was entirely filled and overflowing; did you notice that?" He said, "Yes, I did, and I wondered about it. I wondered how you did it." I said, "Well, I'll tell you how I did it: I did it by charging them, that's how. If I were running a church, I think probably I'd place a price on each pew, and make them pay." The trouble with the churches is that they let 'em get away without paying.

Everything that's worthwhile in this world, ladies and gentlemen, should have a price upon it, and does have a price upon it, in one way or another. The things that you give away absolutely free, people usually value about as much as they pay for them.

One question—"How do you know?"—is the favorite question of the accurate thinker. When the thinker hears somebody make a statement that he questions as being sound, he immediately says, in his mind or openly and orally to the other man, "How do you know?" If you'll get in the habit of using that little sentence more often, you'll be surprised at how many times you put speakers over the barrel because there are so many people that make statements about things that they can't back up, and they can't give you a satisfactory reason as to how they made the statement, or why. "How do you know?" We don't ask this question often enough.

I was lecturing once on this subject, and one of my listeners who perhaps didn't lean too much toward the religious side said, "Dr. Hill, I don't want to embarrass you." I said, "You go right ahead, my friend. If you can embarrass me, you're really good, because I've not been embarrassed even by experts." He said, "Suppose that I asked you that question, 'How do you know?' and I asked you if you believed in God, that there was a God, and asked you, 'How do you know?' wouldn't you be in a fix?" I said, "My friend, if there is one thing in this universe in connection with which there is more evidence of the existence of than anything else, it is the existence of a God. I wouldn't perhaps describe the God that you describe, I might not call him by the name that you call him by, but I'd be talking about the same thing. Because if you want evidence of a first cause, a planner, an overall plan being carried out, you'll find it in every atom of matter, you'll find it in every planet, in every sun that's floating through our universe. You'll find it in every human being and everything that grows out of the ground, all orderly, going on according to an overall plan. Overall plans, my friend, do not create themselves."

Then I took my wristwatch off, and I said, "I have here a very accurate, dependable watch. If I took this watch apart, took the wheels apart, poured them into my hat and shook them from now until doomsday, they would never reassemble in the form of a watch that would keep time, would they?" He said, "No, they wouldn't." I said, "But if I took them to a watchmaker, who started out with a plan, who understood watches, he could put those wheels back and make them work again, couldn't he?" He said, "Yes, he could." I said, "There is no workable and working thing in the whole universe that does not have intelligence back of it, and that intelligence is what you call God. I call it infinite intelligence." That's my way, ladies and gentlemen, of proving to myself that there is a first cause, and there's plenty of evidence to back it up.

Speaking of being guided by logic as one of the three factors that go into accurate thinking, I want to show you how I applied that in connection with a circumstance some years ago. One of my students came to me with a manuscript of a book, a child's book that she had written. It was a well-written book, and she had very crudely illustrated it with cats and dogs and crows and birds and horses and chickens and things, into whose mouths she had placed the words in the book. In other words, she had these birds and cats and dogs and animals talking to one another, and she'd worked it up into a dialogue. It was really a clever thing. But she had taken these pictures—she cut them out of the Sears Roebucks' catalog and out of the *Ladies' Home Journal* and from here, there, and the other place, and they were very crude. Also, the grammar of her book was very poor. The idea was first-class. She came to me just prior to giving this book to a printer who had sold her on the idea of having a number of copies of it printed, for which he was charging her $2,500. Not having the $2,500, she borrowed $1,500 of it from her relatives, and the other thousand, she had.

When I broke the subject down, I said: "If you allow that printer to have those books printed, all you'll have will be some books that you can store down in the basement. If you want to be an accurate thinker and use logic, you'll go to somebody who'll correct that grammar, an artist who will draw the right kind of drawings, and then you will take the book to an established publisher who has a market for it after the book is printed."

Where did I get that information? I got it from experience that I'd had myself, and from observations of other people who had made the mistake of becoming their own publisher. Logic helped me to save that woman's $2,500, and later I found her a publisher for this book, and she made a lot of money from it.

We will give the next section of this talk on accurate thinking, friends of the radio audience, in the next program, as we have run out of time tonight. Thank you for listening.

4

HOW TO BE AN ACCURATE THINKER

Friends in the radio audience, thanks for tuning in to-night. We're now on the second half of the lesson on accurate thinking. I wish to give you some acid tests to be used in the business of separating facts from erroneous information—this is perhaps the most important part of this entire lesson. Tonight you will learn how to assess and analyze information in order to make decisions, and how to avoid pitfalls to accurate thinking.

First of all, scrutinize with unusual care everything you read in newspapers or hear over the radio, and form the habit of never accepting any statement as fact merely because you read it or heard it expressed by someone. Statements bearing some proportion of fact often are intentionally or carelessly colored to give them an erroneous meaning. If a politician said it, for example, if you want to get at the facts, just reverse what he said, and you'll come very near to the truth. Is that clear enough? Scrutinize carefully everything you read in books, regardless of who wrote them. Never accept the words of any writer without asking at least the following questions, and satisfying yourself as to the answers.

I'll give you the questions in just a moment. But if you were applying this information to my books, and many of you have read them, it would apply just the same as to any other person's books. No matter how much you may think of me, how much confidence you may have in me, there are certain ways and means by which you may test my books, the soundness of them, just as you can test the soundness of anybody else's books or anybody else's statements.

If you are going to pass upon the soundness of my books, however, and you weren't sure in your own mind as to whether or not they were sound, a few statistics would help you very greatly: First of all, the fact that over 65 million people have read my books, and a large percentage of those people have expressed the fact that they were benefited by them. Second, the fact that during the past twenty-four years, the books I have written have grossed over $23,400,000, spread out over two thirds of the civilized world. Third, the fact that the information that went into those books came from five hundred of the most outstanding and successful men this country has ever known. Add the fact that the books, when finished, were passed upon by scientists who made certain that every statement in those books conformed entirely to the principles of science and to the natural laws of the universe. Those facts, plus your own application of logic as you read the books, would give you the answer.

If you wanted to go still further in determining whether my books were sound or not, then you might well make a survey of some people who had read them, and find out specifically what benefits they had received from them, and determine as you made this survey if the books or the philosophy had directly or indirectly at any time ever damaged or injured anyone. That's how you'd go about determining whether my books are sound or not. How many of you have gone about it that way? Well, of course, I didn't expect you to. I expected you to accept me at face value, which most of you have done. But if you really and truly wanted to check on me yourselves, that's the way you would go about it.

Here are the steps that you should take in checking up on a writer. First of all, is the writer a recognized authority on the subject he covers? I suppose you know that there are a lot of people who write books about a great many things, and not all of them are capable of writing books, but there's no law against it. If they can get the money with which to publish a book, print a book, or find a publisher willing to take a chance, there's nothing to hinder anybody from writing on the subject he chooses. I judge from the books I have seen that there are a lot of people writing on many subjects that don't have enough information to write accurately on those subjects.

Second, did the writer have an ulterior or a self-interest motive, other than that of imparting accurate information, when he wrote the book you are examining? You know that people never do anything without a motive. If you understand the motive, which prompts a man to write a book or to make a speech or to make a statement, you'll come very near determining whether his statements, whether written or spoken, are accurate or merely guesswork, or merely opinions without proper research.

Third, you should ask the question, is the writer a paid propagandist whose profession is that of organizing public opinion? In these last twenty or twenty-five years that word "propaganda" has come to be so generally in use, and it's done so much damage all over this world, that it behooves any person who wishes to be an accurate thinker to look carefully into any statement made by any person reflecting negatively upon the worth of our country, our form of government, our American way of life, or anything that concerns us as Americans. It behooves us to look with particular interest into the backgrounds of all such people.

There are many of them expressing themselves in print, some of them very forcefully, some of them very well educated, able writers, some of them very able teachers in our colleges and universities, some of them in our churches, in the pulpits, able clergymen, indirectly and subtly teaching a philosophy, the object of which is to overthrow our great American way of life. The gullible people that have swallowed that kind of argument, it's almost unbelievable that they would have done it. They have, in a great many instances, become gullible innocently and honestly, because they didn't take the time to check into the background of the man doing the talking or the writing, they didn't analyze what he said, and consequently, they accepted the opinions of other people.

The next question to ask is, has the writer a profit interest, or other interest in the subject on which he writes, which might have influenced him to make statements that were not accurate? Where money's involved, oftentimes men can slant the truth considerably in their favor. Of course, that doesn't happen among you businessmen, or professional men, in the studio audience. You stick strictly to the truth. You're selling beans, and the customer wants to know if there are any rotten ones in the barrel, you tell them, "Why sure, there are a lot of them in there, but there are a lot of sound ones, too." Or do you?

I stopped on the roadway down near Salem, Illinois,

last week and bought a nice, big sack of grapefruit. It was a lovely sack, that is, the part that we could see on top. But when we got home, we found the entire layer on the bottom side of it, the side the seller didn't show us, was rotten. So I just loaded that sack right back into my car, and when I go back to Salem next week, I'm going to take it back and make him a present of it, and tell him I'd like to see him start eating the grapefruits while I'm there, and start with the lower row—the ones he didn't show us. You wouldn't think a businessman would do a thing like that, but some of them do. They take the easy way, the dishonest way, the path of least resistance for the undisciplined man, and, like all rivers, they end up crooked.

Next, is the writer or the speaker a person of sound judgment, and not a fanatic on the subject on which he writes or speaks? There are a lot of fanatics loose in this world today. I suspect you hear them on the radio every now and then. They write books, too, sometimes. And if you're going to be influenced by that type of thinking, you of course can't class yourself as an accurate thinker, nor anything even approaching accurate thinking. You're allowing some fellow to reach you through emotions, overcome your reason, and get you to accept his ideas. Sometimes those ideas are not injurious, and sometimes they are. A fanatic, you know, oftentimes gets a great kick out of expressing his fanaticism just to see other people wiggle and get excited. He doesn't intend to take anything away from them; he just intends to get them stirred up.

Next, are there reasonably accessible sources from which the writer or the speaker may be checked and verified? Reasonable sources. When I first announced my plans to come into this community, there were a great many people who hadn't heard of me before, who had never read my books. There was no reason for them to be passing judgment upon me one way or another, yet some of them did, until they made some investigation, checked into my background, checked into the record of my books, and at least some of them read the books. The ones who did the most criticizing were the ones who knew nothing about me, had never read my books, and had no information upon which to go. Who were the ones who did that marvelous thinking about me? Why, they were the ones from the other side of the railroad tracks, the ones who really needed this philosophy most, but they'll never be able to get it. I hope they're listening in on this program, some of them. You who did check into my background found out what I'd been doing for the past thirty-five, forty years. You passed judgment upon the philosophy itself in the final analysis, and you found it sound. You found that it worked wherever you applied it. In other words, you used accurate thinking.

Next, ascertain the writer's or the speaker's reputation

for veracity. I suppose you know that not all people have good reputations for veracity. Especially that would apply in politics. If you're going to be influenced by politicians at all, just remember that of all of the professions in this world where truth is lacking most, it's in the field of politics. It used to be, back when I was a youngster growing up, that if a man were a politician—let us say if he were a congressman—he was looked up to with respect. But nowadays, if you call a man a politician, you're liable to find yourself faced with a slander suit. Politics has come to mean a disgraceful, disreputable, unjust, unfair system of trying to get into office not on your own merits, but on the other fellow's demerits. That's a peculiar type of salesmanship, and a peculiar type of thinking.

Of course, there are exceptions to that rule. There are politicians who do not and would not resort to that. But the majority of them do. For that reason, you the voters, I and you owe it to ourselves and to our fellow men in dealing with politicians not to be influenced by any politician who tries to get into office by trying to tear the other fellow down.

Next, learn to be cautious and to use your own judgment, no matter who is trying to influence you. If a statement does not harmonize with your own reasoning power, and if it is out of kilter with your experience and logic, at least hold it up for further examination. Don't move on it until you get more information. Falsehood has a queer way of bringing with it some form of warning note, perhaps in the tone of the voice of the one bringing it. This, when it is recognized, is known as intuition. Isn't that a strange thing, that falsehood has a queer way of bringing with it, in whatever form it's expressed, a warning note?

I can truthfully tell you that in all of my life, despite the number of people in whom I have been disappointed, I have never been fooled by anyone about anything. Oftentimes, for instance, in employing business managers—I've had about ten business managers—and they nearly all went bad. They were more interested in doing me for something than they were doing something for me. In those instances, that warning note came when I was interviewing these managers before I employed them. But I was in need of a man, and I took the nearest man at hand, not because I had full confidence in him, but because I hoped that my inner warning would turn out to be false, and that he would be all right. But it rarely did work out that way.

If you'll watch yourself in business transactions and in social situations, you'll find that a warning note always comes with the falsehood. I can't tell you how to detect it; you can only tell that yourself. Women usually know more about that than men. I've heard it said that in courtship, women don't pay so much attention to what men say as they do to the way they say it. Is that correct, ladies, or not? I think it is correct. It's not so much what the man says, it's the way he says it that telegraphs to the woman, women having a much keener sense of intuition than men, whether the man is lying or trying to make a good impression, or whether he's sincere.

When I want to find out about men, I always take my wife, Annie Lou, along with me. She has a very keen sense of intuition. I connive to turn her loose with the man about whom I wish to know a great deal, and let her talk with him a little while. She always comes back and gives me the lowdown on him. I've never known her to be wrong about it.

Most women have a very keen sense of intuition, but many women don't always allow themselves to be guided by that sense of intuition. They very often override it. When they do, they generally get into trouble. I think you can confirm that, too, ladies.

In seeking facts from others, and here is a humdinger, do not disclose to them what facts you wish to find because many people have the habit of trying to please, even if they have to fabricate or exaggerate. You stop any person you wish and ask that person the way to some small, out of the way place, and he'll point right down the road and say, "Well, it's right down there, about two miles, and then you turn to the right two miles, and then you go two miles farther on, and there it is." As a matter of fact, it might be that the place is back in the other direction, but he will never tell you that he doesn't know. He'll always give you the information.

Most people are like that: They don't want to admit that they don't know. When they find out what answer you expect, there is a common trait, a common weakness, in people to try to give you the answer you're looking for. Remember that. Remember that if you really and truly wish information, don't give the person from whom you are seeking it the slightest idea as to what you think he's going to say. Then he, having nothing to guide him, will slip up and maybe give you the truth.

This all comes under the heading of accurate thinking. Science is the art of organizing and classifying facts. When you wish to make sure you're dealing with facts, seek scientific sources for their testing wherever possible. Men of science have neither a reason nor the inclination to modify or change facts, nor to misrepresent. The scientists are the most accurate thinkers in the world, because they are searching for whatever is there, not for what they would like to find there.

When Madame Curie started out in search of radium, when nobody knew what radium was like, they didn't know how many molecules to the atom, they didn't know where to look for it; she started out with an open mind.

If she hadn't had an open mind, she never would have discovered the existence of radium. She went on the hypothesis through inductive reasoning that there must be a metal known as radium, and by following certain principles of science she eventually isolated that metal and brought it into captivity.

Another thing about accurate thinking: Your emotions are not always reliable. As a matter of fact, they're generally ninety-five percent unreliable. That has to do with all of your emotions, negative and positive. Before being influenced too far by your feelings, give your head a chance to pass judgment on the business at hand. The head is more dependable than the heart. The person who forgets this generally regrets it.

Here are some of the major enemies of sound thinking: At the head of the list—you would never guess this— but at the head of the list, the most outstanding enemy of accurate thinking is the greatest of all the emotions, the emotion of love. If you're going to be an accurate thinker, you'll have to tie a string on each end of your heart and hold on to both of those strings at all times. If you fall down in your overzealous expression of the emotion of love, be sure that you don't let loose of both of those strings, that you at least hold on to one of them. Some people, when they give way to the feeling of love, they go off the deep end, they go overboard, and some of them never come up for air. It's pitiful, isn't it, that the greatest of all the emotions can be and often is the most dangerous of all.

The emotion of love is never dangerous to an accurate thinker. In all of my life—and I have had plenty of love affairs, you may be sure of that; might as well confess it now—I've had plenty of them. But in all of my life, I never got hurt but once, and I don't think I ever hurt anybody but once. The time that I got hurt was when I went off the deep end and forgot to hold on to that other string. I went overboard completely, and it cost me. It cost me at least a million dollars in cash; that's quite an item. Fortunately, I had the wherewithal to pay up. But that was nothing in comparison with the sorrow and the grief and what it did to me. It took me five years to recover, to get back to where I started from. This is a part of my background that you haven't heard about, I guess. But you might as well hear it, and you might as well know that it can happen to anybody. With all of my ability to use self-discipline, I overlooked because I chose to overlook. I wanted to have one love experience in my life with a dangerous person, and ladies and gentlemen, I had it. And I want to tell you something more: It was worth it. It was worth it because I recovered and learned from it.

Honest, confession is good for the soul. It's worth it

in many ways. First of all, I learned not to do it again. Second, I learned that I was strong enough, despite the fact that I had given way to the most outstanding and influencing of the emotions, to regain my equilibrium and my reasoning. It would be impossible for anybody to come along and play that trick on me again. As a matter of fact, nobody played it on me; I played it on myself. I jumped off the deep end. I wanted to see what it was like. I'd had every other experience, practically. I wanted to see what it was like to be let down in a love affair—and brother, I got it. A million dollars' worth.

Some of the other major enemies of accurate thinking are hatred and anger and jealousy and fear and revenge and greed and vanity and egotism and the desire for something for nothing and procrastination. You'll never do any accurate thinking when you're angry—just remember that. You'll never be an accurate thinker as long as you allow any of these emotions, the constructive, the positive, or the negative, to take possession of you. Accurate thinking is a very cold-blooded business, ladies and gentlemen. Very cold-blooded. It's done with your head, not with your heart.

I wouldn't want to be a person who didn't give expression to his heart; why, I'd be a human automaton. I don't mean that you should shut off your finer emotions, nor any of your emotions entirely, but I do say that you can use self-discipline to keep all of those emotions under control at all times. When it comes to the point at which you need to be cold-blooded in order to think and to deal with facts instead of letting your emotions rule you, that's when you want to put on the pressure of self-discipline, and let your head do the thinking, not your heart.

Love is the greatest thing in the world, beyond any question of a doubt. There would be no civilization without it. Man would be nothing but an animal without it. By the same token, it's the most dangerous of all of the emotions if you are not an accurate thinker. I suspect there are people in this audience who could say amen to that.

Then there is religious fanaticism—that's an enemy to accurate thinking. If you do not approach your religion by the more practical means of determining its soundness and its usefulness to you, if you approach it from the viewpoint of the fanatic, you'll never be an accurate thinker.

In politics, fanaticism is detrimental to accurate thinking. I happen to have had the privilege of working very closely with Franklin D. Roosevelt during his first term as president. There were some of us in his confidence who believed that he was sent direct from heaven during that first term. Then again, there were some others who believed that he came from another place. And in each case, the thinking was not necessarily based upon knowledge of the man so much as it was the way they felt about what he was doing. Fanaticism. And if you want to find it rampant, you'll find it in the field of religion and in the field of politics, more than in any other place. And next to that, in the field of economics.

The only thing over which you have complete control is the power of thought. Do not give up this prerogative right to anyone, for any purpose whatsoever. Uncontrolled enthusiasm and imagination are also dangerous to the business of thinking accurately. Keep a close watch on these two especially. They are dangerous when not under your control.

It's a wonderful thing to have enthusiasm; as a matter of fact, I don't know anything great that was ever accomplished without enthusiasm behind it. It's a marvelous thing to have an imagination, to picture a thing mentally before you create it or before you see it in its physical form. If it had not been for enthusiasm and imagination, the great American way of life as we know it today, with all of our conveniences, all of our riches, would not be in existence. The Indians would still be here running this country—and maybe it wouldn't be such a bad idea, after all, if they were. That's where you're supposed to applaud.

Last but not least, to be an accurate thinker let your mind be an eternal question mark. Question everything

and everyone until you satisfy yourself that you are dealing with facts. Do this quietly, in the silence of your
own mind, and avoid being known as a doubting Thomas.
Be a good listener, but also be an accurate thinker as you
listen.

I see that we are out of time. Thank you, and good
night.

5

APPLIED FAITH

How do you do, ladies and gentlemen? Thank you for being with me again today. Our subject on today's show, and on our next broadcast, is applied faith. I want to tell you in the beginning that it has no reference whatsoever to orthodox religion. I'm not approaching it from that angle. Faith is a state of mind which must be cultivated by some technique which will help the individual to take full possession of his own mind at all times and for all purposes, and to be able to direct it to any desire, with the belief that this end will be obtained. That word "belief," ladies and gentlemen, is the key word to this entire principle.

I don't know whether you've ever read that book called *The Magic of Believing* by Claude Bristol or not. If you haven't read it, I would strongly recommend that you get it. It will be well worth your time because it gives a very fine slant on this subject of belief and what you may expect as a result of it.

Faith is one's power to contact and to use infinite intelligence with hypnotic intensity. Don't become alarmed at that word "hypnotic" because, whether you recognize it or not, you're making use of hypnotism all your life. Generally speaking, most people use it in a negative way to hypnotize themselves into fear and self-imposed limitations instead of faith. Consequently they never get very far.

Here are some of the factors that go into the development of this thing called faith: To begin with it starts with a definite purpose, fixing your mind upon some objective or something that you wish to obtain, and then developing behind that objective a burning desire. A burning desire is something very different from a hope or a wish. We all have hopes and wishes; we'd like to have a lot of money without working for it, we hope to be famous, we hope to be recognized, we hope to have good health, but that isn't what I'm talking about in connection with applied faith. I'm talking about a burning desire placed behind some definite objective with the belief that you're going to obtain that objective.

I used to teach my students to go into a quiet room, take their written major purpose or their minor purposes with them, read them aloud, and then look at themselves in a mirror and affirm that they are going to obtain those objectives, whatever they happen to be. Not a bad idea to follow.

Second, a positive mind free from all negatives such as fear, envy, hatred, jealousy, and greed is absolutely essential to the development of faith. You cannot give space in your mind to envy, or greed, or fear, or jealousy, or any of the other negatives, and at the same time make use of the principle of applied faith.

I wonder if you know, my friends, why the majority of prayers never result in anything except a negative result. Had you ever stopped to think about that? Had you ever stopped to wonder why, generally speaking, your prayers are not answered? You must have observed that that's true. Well, I want to tell you something that may be shocking. All prayers are answered. They are answered to correspond precisely with the state of mind in which you utter them. Generally speaking, when we pray we only go to prayer after everything else has failed and we're half scared to death anyway, and we half believe, or more than half believe, that whatever we pray for we're not going to get. And I suspect that sometimes we pray for things that we're not entitled to and we know it. We may not like the answer, but these prayers receive the answers they deserve.

The next factor essential to the development of faith is a mastermind alliance with one or more people who radiate courage based on faith and are suited mentally and spiritually to one's needs in carrying out a given purpose. It's absolutely necessary if you're going to make full and free use of the principle of applied faith to align yourself with one or more people who will work with you in a spirit of harmony, who have a fine influence upon you.

I remember back in the early days when I was struggling to get recognition and to get a start and to find a publisher who would publish my philosophy, there was one man in the United States who had such a fine positive influence upon me that very often I would go all the way down to Florida to have a day or two's visit with him. That man was Edwin C. Barnes, the only partner that Thomas A. Edison ever had. I could sit down and talk with Mr. Barnes and he'd slap me on the back and tell me that I could do anything I made up my mind to do, and in a little while he'd sell me that idea. When I started to believe it I found out that I could do it.

There is a motto in connection with this lecture which I hope that you will get into your notes, but more important you will get into your mind. That motto is that whatever the mind can conceive and believe the mind can achieve. There are three key words in that sentence. Those three key words are conceive, believe, and achieve. A lot of people can conceive ideas, can lay out plans, but they don't believe sufficiently in their ability to carry them out, and consequently negative results happen.

Next, to develop faith there must be recognition of the fact that every adversity carries with it the seed of an equivalent benefit. Unless and until you accept that principle, understand it, and begin to profit by it, you will not make the most of the principle of applied faith. The circumstances of life are such that no matter who you are or what you're doing or how meritorious your efforts may be, you're going to meet with adversities and defeats and disappointments and setbacks. Everybody meets with them but in every such circumstance, ladies and gentlemen, there is a seed of equivalent benefit, and you must have faith that that is so.

Let me give you an illustration. Last fall I came over from our home in California and put on an advertising campaign in the city of St. Louis. I spent a considerable sum of money, around I should say $6,000, and for the first time in my life the class lecture receipts were not as much as we had spent for advertising. We went in the hole about $5,500. You would say that would be an adversity. I think you would call it that, or even defeat. But I didn't accept that setback as defeat. I said to my workers and associates in connection with that campaign, it makes not the slightest difference whether we make money or lose money, in the overall picture this is just a part of what we're doing and out of it will come some good.

Let me call your attention to one thing that came out of it. A man from Paris saw our advertisement, came over to St. Louis, and twisted my arm as he calls it, brought me over to Paris, and out of my contact with him has grown this marvelous movement that's going to send this philosophy forward by leaps and bounds. If I had deliberately planned to come over here to Paris and to organize this radio series and to make it a means of carrying this philosophy to the people, I couldn't have done a better job, and all of that came unexpectedly out of that one failed campaign. I don't know but I suspect there will be other benefits that will come out of it, too, but that alone has more than paid off already. We're not in the red over here in Paris.

Next, there must be a habit of affirming one's definite major purpose or one's minor purposes in the form of a prayer, at least once daily. It makes no difference what your religion may be. You certainly have some form of prayer, some method of praying. You must believe in prayer, and if you will take your prayers and place them definitely behind your major objective in life and enter into those prayers each day with the belief that they're going to be fulfilled, you will find that certain changes will take place in your mental attitude. They will attract to you the necessary things and people and circumstances to carry out the object of those prayers or that dominant major aim, whatever it may be.

My method works while I'm asleep just the same as when I'm awake. I call it my eight princes. The reason I get such marvelous results from these eight princes, all of whom of course are self-made by me, is that I believe in them. I expect that they are going to work for me. I expect that the prince of financial prosperity is going to keep me supplied with all the finances I need, and up until the present time he's much more than done that, I can assure you. He's a pretty nice fellow to have around, too. I want to tell you that.

And the prince of sound physical health . . . he's done all right by me. Of course, last week you know that he did let me down a little bit. I got sick and missed a broadcast. But I got after him and we had a nice heart-to-heart talk and he promised me that if I would be real careful that he wouldn't let me down again so that I missed my show as I did on that Friday night. Incidentally, that's the first time in my whole career that I've missed a show on account of physical health, because I have this marvelous system, this marvelous talisman who looks after my health, and he does a perfect job of it.

The next one is the prince of peace of mind. I don't know of anything in this world that's more necessary or more important to people than to have peace of mind. It makes no difference how much money you have or how much success you may attain or how much fame you may gain, if you don't have peace of mind along with it, you are indeed poor. I would go so far as to say that the major objective of this philosophy is to help people acquire the formula by which they may attain and retain peace of mind. I don't mean just occasionally but continuously.

Next, to develop applied faith one must recognize the existence of infinite intelligence, which gives orderliness to the entire universe. One must recognize that the individualities and minute expressions of this intelligence, and as such of the individual mind, have no limitations except those set up in one's own mind. Is that a marvelous thing to recognize and to know? There are no limitations to the use of a mind except those which you set up in your own mind or permit the circumstances of life to set up for you. You can bowl over every circumstance of life that limits your ability to think if you make up your mind to do it.

It seems to me that when you stop to consider that the Creator gave man complete control over but one thing, that the Creator must have intended that that was the most important thing in the world. How strange it is, my friends, that civilization has not included in its education and religions the importance of this marvelous gift from the Creator, a gift so powerful that it enables one to practically proclaim and carry out one's own earthly destiny. That gift, need I remind you again, is the control that you have over your own mind; the ability to make it negative or positive; the ability to think in big terms or in little terms; the ability to establish your own pattern as to what you want in life and to make life pay off on your own terms, or to accept the circumstances of life and allow life to ride you.

I've often compared life to a horse because life is something you can ride if you will, but if you don't watch it, the horse will do the riding and you will play horsey. You have to make up your mind which it's going to be.

Personally I have never accepted from life anything that I didn't want. I have no intention of doing it in the future. When my son, Blair, was born without any ears, without hearing, I never accepted that circumstance. I said I know something about the power of faith, I know something about the use of the subconscious mind, and I started in immediately to build a pattern through which this child would receive an improvised hearing aid of some nature that would enable him to hear normally. I could easily have accepted the condition when the doctors told me that my child would be a deaf and dumb mute all of his life. I could easily have accepted that condition as being the last word and have forgotten about it. I could easily have started in to have him taught the lip-reading language or the finger

sign language of the deaf and dumb, but I didn't want him
to understand or know there was any such thing as that.

I immediately went to work on him in a spirit of faith
knowing that there was nothing impossible, that whatever
the mind could conceive and believe the mind could
achieve, and in nine years' time I did influence nature to
improvise for him hearing equipment that gave him sixty-
five percent of his normal hearing.

I've had such marvelous experiences, my friends, in un-
doing the circumstances that people call the impossible
through applied faith that I know something of its power.
I couldn't begin to describe to you, in terms that would
perhaps influence you to the fullest extent, the great capacity that you have to use your own mind for whatever purpose you wish to use it and to attain that purpose.

Every living thing that comes into this world lower
than the order of man has its destiny fixed for it by what
we call instinct. Its pattern is already laid out and it cannot go one step beyond that pattern. Man has no pattern
except that which he builds for himself. It can be large or
it can be small, it can be great or it can be insignificant.
Man controls his own earthly destiny if he will use the
power the Creator gave him, and do it in the spirit of
belief that he can carry out his own ends.

I suggest you take a careful inventory of your past defeats and adversities from which it will become obvious

that all such experiences do carry the seed of an equivalent benefit. You will realize that I am right about this.

Now let us go into the subject of how to create a mental attitude favorable for the expression of faith, a mental attitude because, after all is said and done, applied faith is nothing but a mental attitude, and you control your mental attitude. That's the only thing in fact that you do control. You don't control your wife, gentlemen—you know that. You don't control your bank account always. But you do control your own mental attitude. You can make it whatever you choose.

First of all, in making your mental attitude favorable for the expression of faith, you must know what you want, become determined in your own mind that you're going to get it, and decide what you're going to give in return for it. Nature frowns upon the idea of getting something for nothing. I know I don't recommend it. There are some people in the world, I understand, who would like to have things without paying for them, but that is no part of this philosophy.

Second, when you affirm the object of your desires through prayer, let your imagination see yourself already in possession of it. You may think that's difficult to do. I had a student some years ago who needed a thousand dollars very badly and he came to see me about how to get it. He had to have this thousand dollars within a week's time. I said, "Sit down and take out your checkbook and write yourself out a check for a thousand dollars." He said, "That won't do any good, the check's no good." I said, "Well, it will soon be good, write it out payable to cash one week from today."

He did as I told him and then he went to work on his own mind, and two days later he called me up and said that he had received from an unexpected source $1,500 in cash. In other words, he had $500 more than he needed. He said, "I'm going to go down and cash that check." And he did, and he has it framed and hanging in his library today, because that was the beginning of his first real recognition of the fact that when you believe in a thing, when you take steps to carry it out as if it already had been accomplished, it puts the power of infinite intelligence squarely back of you.

Next, when you're overtaken by defeat, as you will be many times, no doubt, remember that man's faith is tested many times and your defeat may be only one of your testing times. If you don't take anything away from this particular broadcast except this thought, just remember whenever you're defeated or disappointed or suffer frustration of any kind, you are probably under the spotlight being tested to see whether you're a man or a mouse.

We do go through testing times. I went through twenty

years of them while I researched and developed this philosophy, and if I hadn't been able to stand up under the test of failure and defeat I would have never given the world the great collection of success principles that I have given it, which now serves millions of people.

I would say that the best part of my experience came not out of my successes but out of my failures, because I survived those failures. I made up my mind that they meant nothing in my life except the challenge to greater effort, and that's the attitude that you've got to take toward defeat because you are going to have these testing times. As a matter of fact, I'm very glad to know that I did go through many major failures, because I now recognize that the average person would have fallen down under the first one or two. I found out that there is nothing in the world that can floor me and keep me floored.

How did I find it out? I found it out because I have a formula for dealing with the subject of failure and it applies under all circumstances. I don't care how hard the going is, how many gossipers talk, how many people criticize, I go right on doing business at the same old stand, and the philosophy goes marching on. Why? Because I don't quit when the going is hard, when there are obstacles in my path. I strongly recommend that you take up that policy and carry it out. This is yet another example of persevering, of not giving up, of not following that path of least resistance taken by all rivers and some drifting men.

Next, any negative state of mind will destroy the power of faith and result in a negative conclusion. Your state of mind is everything: you must have a burning desire.

Let's find out what is a burning desire. What do I mean by a burning desire? A burning desire is a purpose so definitely fixed in your mind that you take it to bed with you at night, you get up with it in the morning, you have it wake you up during the night probably, you talk about it, you think about it, you eat with it, you sleep with it, and you get it, and later it gets you. And when it gets you, you really have a burning desire. A burning desire is such a determined effort to accomplish a certain end that no matter how many setbacks or frustrations you meet with, you keep right on going. That's what a burning desire is. And it is pretty close to this thing which we call applied faith.

There is one thing to avoid when acting on this burning desire. Nature frowns upon all efforts of individuals that work a hardship or an injustice upon others. If you engage in any form of effort based upon your faith which results in damaging or injuring another person, you may be sure that your efforts will come to naught sooner or later.

You may be aware that my most infamous student, and perhaps the most infamous man in the whole world, was Adolf Hitler. When he became a follower of mine I didn't know who Hitler was. I autographed a set of books to him in 1930, long before his intentions were known. Later on he took from that philosophy the fifteen principles that gave him power, the power-making principles, and he ignored the two principles designed to give him moral guidance in the use of that power. And what happened to Hitler? I don't need to go into that. He came within an inch of destroying civilization. I want to warn you against the neglect of those two principles he cast aside, going the extra mile and the golden rule, which were placed there specifically for the purpose of giving you moral guidance in the use of the power that will come out of these other principles.

Well, folks, I see that our time is up for today. Please join me next time for further discussion of applied faith.

6

APPLIED FAITH SUCCESS STORIES

Hello again, ladies and gentlemen. Tonight we will continue our discussion of the important principle of applied faith.

I want to give you some illustrations, my friends, of how this principle of applied faith works out in the practical affairs of life. In doing my research, starting in 1908 at Andrew Carnegie's request, I had the good fortune to be associated with the late Dr. Alexander Graham Bell, the inventor of the long-distance telephone; Mr. Thomas A. Edison; and Dr. Elmer R. Gates, an outstanding scientist living at the time in Chevy Chase, Maryland. These three men, for many years before I ever had the privilege of meeting them and working with them, had made extensive researches into this peculiar phenomenon known as the subconscious mind. They had made outstanding discoveries, and I want to call your attention in particular to the discoveries of Dr. Elmer R. Gates.

When I first went to see Dr. Gates his secretary said, "I'm sorry, but Dr. Gates is sitting for ideas right now and he cannot be disturbed." I said, "I beg your pardon?" She said, "He is sitting for ideas." I said, "What does that mean?" She said, "Well, you'll have to wait for Dr. Gates to come out and have him tell you. It's too much for me." I waited for about two hours and when he came out I repeated the conversation I'd had with his secretary. He said, "Would you like to see how I go about sitting for ideas?" I said, "Certainly I would, Doctor."

He took me back into a room, a specially built room which was soundproofed and was so designed that he could cut off practically all sound and all light. This room was about a ten-foot-by-ten-foot room. It had in it a small wooden table over which there was an electric push button and an electric light and a small chair in front of it and a large stack of paper and pencils. He explained to me that when he wanted to complete a design of a technical nature or work out a patent or work out an unknown problem of any kind, he went into this room, focused his mind upon the known factors of his problem, and demanded that his subconscious mind reveal to him the unknown solutions. He then turned off the lights and waited for results.

Sometimes he'd wait two or three minutes and the ideas would begin to flow, and he would turn on his lights and begin to write. Sometimes he'd wait for an hour or two and get no results, but he said that the results came approximately eighty-five percent of the time. On one occasion he wrote for three hours, and when he examined his notes he had the answer to a scientific problem which he had been pursuing for some ten years without success.

Dr. Gates has to his credit more patents than Mr. Edison, far and away. He was not as well publicized as Mr. Thomas A. Edison. He used to go down to the patent office in Washington to look over the patents that had been filed, and he recognized that some of them were sound on paper but wouldn't work in the laboratory. He would take those patents and go into his silent room, concentrate his mind upon the unknown factors, and come out with the answer and an improved patent. In that way he developed over 250 patents. I think perhaps he was one of the most outstanding men that I have ever known. He recognized how possible and how practical it was to fix his mind upon the things that he wanted and to keep his mind there until infinite intelligence began to yield him up the answers.

I was lecturing to the students at the Harvard University Business School some years ago and I made the statement that the ether is so sensitive that perhaps here in this room where I'm speaking now there are other personalities present if we could only tune in on them and hear them. I didn't get much farther than that until the students broke out into a laugh. They gave me the horse laugh because radio had not been developed at that time. Of course you and I know now that here in this room where I'm speaking I'm in competition with bands, singers, dancers, maybe Edgar Bergen and Charlie McCarthy. I'm in competition with a lot of other intelligences that we know are here in this room.

Every brain is a receiving station for the vibrations of thought. That's well established. There's no doubt about that and many of these thoughts that you are bothered with, negative thoughts, that you find crowding upon you from day to day, do not originate from your own mind but from outside minds, and you maybe haven't yet learned ways and means of immunizing yourself against them.

In connection with this broadcast on how to succeed using applied faith, you must learn to shut out of your mind all of these unpleasant thoughts that can do you no good and can do you a great deal of harm. You've got to learn to do that. You've got to give yourself immunity against all thoughts that are not helpful to you, because when the Creator gave you control over your mind, he intended, I am certain, that you would use that mind for constructive ends and not for destructive ends.

Mr. Edison, while he was working on the incandescent electric lightbulb, was making use all the time of applied faith, and had he not understood that principle, he would have quit a long time before he discovered the answer to his problem. As a matter of fact, as I have told you before, Mr. Edison failed over ten thousand times before he finally discovered the secret of the incandescent lightbulb.

Can you imagine anybody going at anything and failing ten thousand times over a period of years and still sticking by it? Could you do it? Do you have any idea, my friends, how many times the average person has to fail in anything before he makes up his mind that maybe in the first place he didn't want to do that thing, but something else? Give a guess. Give a guess, anybody. How many times? Once? As a matter of fact it doesn't average one time because fifty percent of the people or more quit before they start. They anticipate that they are going to fail and they don't even make a beginning.

That's how much applied faith the majority of people have. They quit before the going even commences to be hard. Mr. Edison was regarded throughout the world as a genius, and the thing that made him a genius more than everything else was his capacity to know what he wanted and to keep his mind fixed on what he wanted until he got it. That's all there is to it, ladies and gentlemen. I don't know why he was forced to go through ten thousand failures, but I do know one thing, that that probably was the source of his greatness, because that was his first great invention. Had he not stuck by these ten thousand testing times that nature put him through, he probably never would have become one of the greatest inventors of all time.

You know everything has a price. If you want to be great in anything you must make up your mind that it has a price. You must find out what that price is and be willing to pay it. Mr. Edison knew that the principle of applied faith would eventually yield him the answer, and when he found it, just listen to this: When he found the answer, he found that it consisted in two well-known principles, both of which he was very familiar with before he started his investigations. All he had to do was to take these two principles and put them together in a new way, marry them so to speak, and lo! there was created the first incandescent electric light. What were those two principles?

First of all he learned, as other experimenters before him had learned, that you could apply electrical energy to a wire or to a piece of metal at the point of friction and you could create a heat, a white heat, and make a light. That was well known. Mr. Edison knew it, others knew it, but the trouble came in that the piece of metal would burn up almost instantly. You couldn't control it. He needed it controlled. After he had failed over ten thousand times he flopped down on his couch in his laboratory and he said to his subconscious mind, "I want to sleep here on this couch until I get the unknown factor, the means of controlling the heat generated by electricity in making an incandescent light."

He told me he had made similar demands upon his subconscious before without anything happening. You see, he was still going through his testing time, the price he had to pay to become a great inventor. When he got up from that nap, as he came out of his sleep, the answer came. It consisted in the charcoal principle. You know that if you take a pile of wood, put it on the ground, and set it afire and cover it over with dirt, it will smolder along until it burns away a large portion of that wood, leaving the charred stick which we call charcoal. The reason the stick doesn't burn up entirely is that there is very little oxygen that gets to it. Where there's no oxygen, there can be no combustion. Where there is but little oxygen, there can be but little combustion. There's just enough oxygen percolating through the dirt to allow that stick of wood to burn to a charred condition, but not enough to burn it up.

Edison said, "There it is, that's the thing I've been waiting for." He went into his laboratory, he took this wire that he had been experimenting with, and he put it inside of a bottle. He sealed up the bottle's neck, and with a bicycle pump he pumped out all of the air and all of the oxygen, leaving a vacuum in that bottle around the wire. He then turned on the electrical energy and lo! and behold there was born the first incandescent electric light in the world. It burned for eight and one half hours and was the beginning of this great electrical age without which these marvelous industries that we enjoy now, for example, radio, television, radar, and the automobile, could never have come into existence. They came about as the result of applied faith, applied by a man who had very little formal education, very little schooling, but a great understanding of this gift from the Creator which entitles one to make whatever use one desires of his own thoughts.

Whenever you think of Edison and his greatness, just remember that he became great only because he didn't quit when the going was hard. Once I asked him, I said, "Mr. Edison, what would you have done if on that ten thousandth trial you hadn't found the answer?" He said, "Well, I'll tell you what I would be doing right now, I would be in my laboratory working on the solution instead of fooling away my time talking to you." I think he meant just that. He put everything he had on the determination to find the answer through which he could give the world an incandescent electric light.

Look again, my friends, at how nature works. The very next invention that Mr. Edison went to work on after the incandescent light, after ten thousand failures, was the talking machine. Nobody had ever made a machine that would record and reproduce the sound of the voice. It never had been done, and when Mr. Edison completed that machine he gave the world a new idea. When the idea came to him he took a pencil out of his pocket and an old envelope and on the back of the envelope he drew a crude picture of the first talking machine that would ever be made to work in the world. He turned this drawing over to his pattern maker and told him to make a machine. It consisted of a little cylinder with a crank at the end of it which he could turn, and that cylinder was covered over with some sort of substance, some sort of soft substance, maybe wax. He applied a needle to this wax, a needle fixed to the end of a trumpet, one of these old-fashioned hearing-aid trumpets, and started to crank the thing up with his hand, and it worked the very first time.

In other words, nature has a way of compensating you for these defeats and failures. If you fail today, the chances are you will have acquired something that will enable you not to fail tomorrow. Nature never takes anything away from anyone or allows anything to be taken away without giving to that person something of equivalent or greater value than it took in its place.

Years ago, when I went to work for La Salle Extension University as its first advertising manager, I was faced with a problem that was quite practical and quite sizable. They had no money on which to operate, and I didn't know that until I went to work with them. It's a very essential thing in business to have some money. They had about eighteen thousand students throughout the United States and most of the students were mad at them because the collection manager had been sending them threatening letters. I faced the problem of satisfying eighteen thousand students and also acquiring operating capital that was at least in the neighborhood sufficient for La Salle to pay its debts and, vital to me, to pay my salary. They had so little money that when payday came and I got my check, I rushed over to the bank and had it certified before the other employees got there because I knew if I didn't my check would bounce. That was the condition I found them in.

I remembered also that whenever a thing was just and right, that there was always a way of accomplishing it. I went to work and made a survey of La Salle students and employees and found out where the trouble was. Out of the thirty-five employees that they had at headquarters, twenty of them were working in the collections department writing nasty letters to their students. You can imagine how popular that made them.

I sat down and started writing sales letters to the students, writing them friendly letters, and then after I had made friends out of them, I sold to many of those eighteen thousand students a million dollars' worth of eight percent preferred stock. Inside of sixty days we had a million dollars in the bank and I no longer had to rush over to the bank to have my paycheck certified. We had operating capital. That was the beginning of the great La Salle Extension University, which became and still is the most successful correspondence school in the world.

There were at the head of that school two very outstanding men, one of them a college graduate. They had some very able men there but they were dealing, ladies and gentlemen, with almost every conceivable thing except the thing that would have worked them out of the hole, and that was applied faith. They had caused these eighteen thousand students to lose confidence in them. They had lost confidence in themselves. They had set up, through the wrong use of their mental attitude there in the university, not a drawing card but a repellent force that was carrying them rapidly into bankruptcy.

How many times, oh how many times, have I been called into business institutions where I found that the very fire that was burning up their vitals was being set off by matches carried in the pockets of the men who should have been the salvation of the business, but weren't, because they didn't understand this principle of applied faith, of believing in themselves and other people.

When Ed Barnes went over to see Thomas A. Edison

he went there to become the partner of Edison. Think of it, the partner of the great Thomas A. Edison, and Ed Barnes had so little money that he went there as a stow-away on a freight train and announced that he had come there to go into partnership with Mr. Edison. Almost an unbelievable thing, but ladies and gentlemen, he stayed there on that job for five years sweeping floors, and doing other menial jobs, until the time finally came, his big opportunity came. And he made the grade, and he did become the only partner that Thomas A. Edison ever had.

I know Ed Barnes exceedingly well. He and I have been close personal friends for over thirty-five years. I know his entire story and I know why it is that he is now a multi-millionaire, why he travels all over the world, why he's finally taking things easy. It all dates back to the time when he went to see Edison and he made up his mind that if it took five years or ten years or whatever number of years it took, he was going to stand by until he got just what he went after. He told me that when he first went there all of the other employees laughed at him, and every time they passed him they'd mockingly called him Edison Junior.

Mr. Meadowcroft, Edison's secretary when Barnes first appeared there and said he was going into partnership, sar-castically wanted to know whether Barnes was to be the senior partner or the junior partner. Barnes said, "Well, it makes no difference where you start me. I will be on top when I'm through anyway." That was his attitude. If you ever knew Ed Barnes, or if you ever have the good pleasure to meet him, you will recognize that his outstanding quality that differentiates him from the average man is his great capacity for faith in his ability to do whatever he makes up his mind to do. I would say to you, those of you who are close to me, and when I dare to speak in the first person, that if you want to take inventory of all the assets and all of the riches that I possess and pick out the thing that's worth the most, I would say it's my great enduring capacity of faith in my ability to do whatever I start out to do. I recommend it to you as being the most essential of all the success principles: the ability to believe in yourself.

During my research, I became acquainted with the principle of autosuggestion, and I commend its use to you. Start talking to yourself, don't do it out on the street, go in the bathroom but don't talk too loudly in there so that the members of the family understand that you really are not out of your head. Start talking to yourself just as if there was another person inside of you and you were addressing that person.

As a matter of fact, there is another person inside of you. That other self, you have another self, you have the one you see in the glass when you're prettying up your hair or your face, and then you have the one that you never see but you feel him if you get on good terms with him. That other self is the one that I want you to become acquainted with, because he's the one that takes over this principle of applied faith and helps you to carry it out to its logical conclusion of whatever you may undertake.

When I look back to the humble beginnings where I started, down in the mountains of Virginia in illiteracy and in poverty, and see what has been accomplished through my efforts in these past forty-odd years, I know well enough that had I not developed the capacity to believe in my own mind, and to use my own mind for ends desirable to me, that I never could have done the job that I have done. I didn't have the educational advantages, I didn't have the opportunities, I didn't have anything except the mind which the Creator gave me, and the privilege of making that mind whatever I wanted it to be. And fortunately, whether by chance or otherwise, I had the good opportunity to come under the influence of my stepmother, who introduced me to my mind and taught me how to use it, slowly, step by step. Working later with other men who had risen to great stations in life, I found out that they, too, had done so solely by embracing this great factor which the Creator had given them, this ability to control their own minds and direct that ability to the ends of their own choosing.

When it comes to the business of genius, Mr. Edison said, "Perish the idea." He said, "Genius is one tenth inspiration and nine tenths perspiration." I really and truly think he had something there.

Applied faith is the ability to draw upon the thing that the Creator intended you to draw upon and to keep it fixed on the things that you want in life and off the things you don't want. You may be surprised to know that the majority of people go all the way through life with the major portion of this marvelous power focused upon the things they don't want, such as poverty, ill health, loss of love of someone, loss of friends, fear of criticism. My what a humdinger that is, that fear of criticism. Fear of what "they" will say. I better find out who "they" are, or maybe not. "They" have no effect on me, I can assure you.

If you allow your mind to dwell upon the things you don't want, that is exactly what you get, and that is what the majority of the people are getting, the things that they don't want. If you get a good hold on this principle of applied faith you will learn to fix your mind upon the things you do want.

I once asked Henry Ford if he'd ever wanted anything in his life real badly that he didn't get, and with a dry little grin he said, "Only once." He said, "I wanted to marry a redheaded girl that I used to go to high school with, but she married another man, but afterwards I was glad she did." I said, "Was that all?" "Yes," he said. "That was all." I said, "Are you in a position today, Mr. Ford, where you can get anything you desire?" He said, "Anything I desire or its equivalent." He said, "I might not be able to get the building at Forty-second and Broadway in New York, but I can get the one just across the street from it or the one on the other corner or the one on the next street which would do just as well."

I had the privilege of working with Mr. Ford for a long period of years and I pledge you my word of honor that his personality was way below average, his beliefs sometimes were off base, and his schooling was modest. I don't think he even finished high school. It wasn't his education or belief system that made him a great industrial operator, it was his capacity to know what he wanted and his "stubbornness" to stick by it until he got it. I'm using the word "stubbornness" as a quotation because many of his associates said it was just pure darn stubbornness. Whatever it was, it enabled him to take possession of his own mind and to keep it fixed upon what he wanted despite all of the obstacles that he had to overcome. His faith drove him and drove him.

You in the audience are faced with a multiplicity of problems. You're living in an age of problems more than ever before. If you don't have a philosophy to live by you're going to be stuck in these next one or two decades. In that philosophy, at the head of the list, the most important thing of all will be the recognition of your own personal power, your own ability to fix your minds on the circumstances and the things in life that you want and to keep your minds there until you get those things. Do not allow the circumstances of life to push you around and to cause you to quit because the going is hard. As a matter of fact I have never seen the time when the going wasn't hard if you made up your mind that it was. I've never seen the time when the going wasn't easy if I kept my mental attitude right.

I recognize that it's very difficult for a person who is facing major problems, such as they want for money or they want for capital or they want for opportunities, to believe in his ability to do the things he wants to do. But that's the time that you're going through this testing that I speak of, the time that you need to turn on the full power of your imagination and to see yourself already in possession of the things you want. Press on through all obstacles; do not lose control and drift aimlessly.

Isn't it a marvelous thing to recognize that you know what you want, you are so definitely sure that you are going to get it, that you can see yourself already in possession of it? Of course you don't start . . . if you want a million dollars, you don't start spending it until its actually in the bank balance. I hardly need to tell you that. But see yourself in possession of it because you know what you are going to give in return for it, and you know that you are entitled to it, and you are going to stand by your guns until you get what you're entitled to.

When I wanted to start the *Golden Rule Magazine* I needed $100,000 and I didn't have it, but I found ways and means of putting out the *Golden Rule Magazine*, and I made the idea stick because I used applied faith. I got a printer to print the magazine and we sold it on the newsstand, and when the sales returns came back I paid him for the printing and I took what was left. Something like that might be an idea for you. Find that definite major purpose, put the power of faith behind it, and you will not fail.

Thank you for listening tonight. Please join me next time when I will begin a discussion of "the other side of the coin," the major causes of failure.

7

THE FIFTEEN MAJOR CAUSES OF FAILURE

Good evening, ladies and gentlemen, and welcome to our first of two programs on the subject of the causes of failure. As many of you know, I've had the privilege of giving the world its first practical philosophy of success, and in order to give you a philosophy that brings about success to individuals, it's necessary to tell you not only what to do, but what not to do. It's just as important to know the negative side as it is the positive. This broadcast and the next deal entirely with the things one must not do in order to succeed.

There is a law of nature which provides that every adversity, every defeat, every setback, every failure, every heartache, every disagreeable circumstance that you may experience, carries within itself the seed of an equivalent benefit. I didn't say the full-blown flower of benefit, or the ripened fruit, I said only the seed. In order to benefit by that seed, you first have to recognize it, you have to know that it's there. You have to expect it and be looking for it, instead of looking at the adverse side or the negative side of the experience.

Second, you must germinate it through some sort of action, and develop it and make use of it. That is absolutely essential. I think, perhaps, of all of the things that I discovered during my forty-odd years of research in this field of philosophy, nothing to me was more astounding or more surprising than the fact that nature had very cleverly arranged that nothing shall be taken away from anyone without giving him something in return. Nothing which nature gave in the way of an asset to any individual shall ever be taken away from him, for any cause whatsoever, without something of an equivalent benefit being given back to him in return. That great law of compensation was described so effectively by Ralph Waldo Emerson in his book of essays.

There are fifteen major causes of failure that I have discovered, and I'm going to give them to you with a brief comment on each one. The first one is the habit of drifting through life without a definite purpose or a definite plan for attaining it. You may be surprised that ninety-eight out of every hundred people belong in that category, as drifters. They're like goldfish in a bowl: they go round and round, always coming back to the starting point, but never getting anywhere. The reason they don't get anywhere is, first of all, they don't discover this marvelous gift of the mind, which is capable of determining their earthly destiny. Second, if they do discover it, they don't make proper use of it. Drifting. Lacking in singleness of purpose. Lacking a plan for carrying out the purpose. There you have the major reason for all failures in this world.

Number two is unfavorable physical heredities at birth. That's something the individual cannot control, but it has been proved, over and over again, that an unfavorable physical condition at the time of birth need not necessarily be a cause for a permanent failure and defeat. I think I have proved this in the case of my son Blair, who was born without any ears, but who became an outstanding young man, and who finally developed a hearing capacity sixty-five percent of normal. I have observed over and over again that even an affliction of that kind carries with it the seed of an equivalent benefit. In the case of my son Blair, that seed of an equivalent benefit consisted in the fact that people looked upon him with a great deal of sympathy. He didn't have the physical capabilities that the other children had, because of his condition, so he had to work harder to get ahead.

I think about men like the late Charles P. Steinmetz, a

genius if ever there was one, who was born with a curvature of the spine, stoop-shouldered and afflicted. He looked more like an ape than he did a man, but he had that marvelous brain inside of his skull, and he didn't in any way allow that affliction to deter him from becoming an outstanding success as a mathematician and electrical engineer. His physical limitations led him to fully develop his mind. When I see men like that, I recognize that even though one may have been born with an unfavorable physical hereditary background, that need not keep one from benefiting by that very affliction.

Number three as a cause for failure is meddlesome curiosity in connection with other people's affairs. Of course, none of my listeners belong in that category—meddlesome curiosity in connection with other people's affairs. You'd be surprised to know how much brainpower, how many hours of brainpower, are spent every day by millions of people throughout the world, through pure meddlesome curiosity. Or maybe it's not so pure; maybe it's rather impure. Meddlesome curiosity in the affairs of other people. Life is so complex, and there are so many obstacles in it, that if we're going to succeed, if we're going to develop our God-given qualities of mind, we must devote all of our time to things that concern us, and not mess with the affairs of other people, especially when they have no impact on us.

Number four as a cause of failure is the lack of a definite, major purpose as a life goal. A major purpose, now. We all have minor purposes, but most of them are not really purposes; they are hopes and wishes. A hope and a wish is not going to get one very far. We all hope to marry well when we marry. Women hope to marry tall, handsome, dark-haired men with lots of money. Men hope to marry beautiful and charming women with personalities. Sometimes they do, and find out that that doesn't even bring success or happiness.

Men and women hope for success in business or in a profession, for money, for fame, for fortune; they hope for those things, wish for them. But that's not the equivalent of a definite, major purpose. If you're going to succeed in life, you've got to have a major goal, an overall objective, an overall purpose. You've got to put the best of your efforts behind that purpose. The majority of people don't have such an aim, and even those who do oftentimes back it only with hopes and wishes, and not with definiteness.

The fifth major cause of failure is inadequate schooling—inadequate education I should have said, instead of schooling, because schooling and education are two separate and distinct terms. A lot of people think that because they go through the grade schools and high schools, college, get some degrees, that they are educated. Perish the idea. That's not what makes people educated.

As a matter of fact, I discovered some years ago that the word "educate" itself is very much misunderstood by the majority of people, and all of the dictionaries I've ever had the privilege of examining give the wrong definition of the word "educate." They say substantially that it means to impart knowledge. It doesn't mean anything of the kind. The word "educate" comes from the Latin word, if I remember correctly, *educio*, which means to draw out, to develop from within.

To develop what? To develop that which you were born with: a mind. Some of the most successful men I have ever had the privilege of knowing and working with had very little formal schooling. But they did have great educations. Among them are Henry Ford and Thomas A. Edison, two of the outstanding ones that had hardly any schooling, but they did have a great amount of development from within. They developed by recognizing the powers of their own minds, recognizing that the Creator gave man control over but one thing, and that was the right to make his mind do whatever he wanted it to do, negative or positive. That's what makes people educated.

If you're looking for an educated person, you'll have to find a person who has discovered himself. Generally speaking, when you find him, you'll find that he graduated from the greatest of all universities, the one in which I hold a master's degree: the University of Hard Knocks. It's one of the greatest schools upon the face of this earth, and if you can survive it, if you can take the tests and go through it, the chances are that you will become truly an educated person, not merely a schooled person. A schooled person usually is just a person who has a good memory and can remember facts long enough to get by at examination time.

I hope I'm not saying anything that steps upon the toes of any of my schoolteacher listeners, but if I am, I must still claim that I'm telling the truth. It's not the schoolteachers' fault our system is what it is; it's the fault of the school system itself, that people are not taught the real meaning of education, and that we do not have school systems that really educate people. People learn by doing, by knowing, by being put on their own, and by being introduced to themselves, to that other self, the one you do not see when you look into a mirror. A lot of people believe when they look at themselves in the mirror that they see themselves, the real self. They don't see anything at all. They only see the house in which the real self lives. If they discover that other self, and make use of it as the Creator intended, the chances are they'll become educated and, consequently, successful.

The sixth cause of failure is lack of self-discipline, generally manifesting itself through excesses in eating, drinking, and sex, and indifference toward opportunities for self-advancement. Lack of self-discipline. What does self-discipline mean? It means that you'll take entire control of your own mind, and make it do whatever you want it to do, instead of being influenced by the minds of your neighbors or those nearest to you, or by those who criticize you. That's what self-discipline means. It means you will run your own life. That doesn't suit a lot of people.

There are some people who want to run the lives of others for them. That very often happens in families: Some member of the family will want to run the lives of every person there. I was brought up in a family somewhat like that myself. But fortunately I kicked over the traces. I was a very bad boy, and I'm glad that I was. I was so bad that I listened to no one, and I didn't allow my father or anybody else to control me. I did my own thinking. It wasn't very good thinking in the beginning, but I finally got straightened out, and drew a bead on the things that make for success in life. I wouldn't have done that if I hadn't had some self-discipline. I had some criticism down through the years, too. I had self-discipline enough not to pay any attention to that, to criticism.

Number seven is lack of ambition to aim above mediocrity. There's one of the outstanding causes of failures: lack of the ambition to aim above mediocrity. People come into the world without their consent. They spend a little time going to school, and they take a job. What kind of job? Why, any kind of job they can make a living from. A job that they like? No, not necessarily, but they have to eat and they have to sleep under a roof, and have to wear a few clothes. They go all the way through life, never aiming at anything other than just enough merely to keep soul and body together, and practically always, that's just about how much they get out of life. Now and then, a man or woman will step out of the line and say, "I'm aiming for a goal way beyond anything that any of my people attained." If that person stands by that goal and lives to see its achievement, it is a rare feat to be applauded.

Number eight is ill health, generally due to wrong thinking, improper diet, and lack of exercise. Ill health can be a cause for failure. But if you live right and you eat right and exercise right and think right, the chances are that you'll not be bothered with ill health. Most ailments are due to bad thinking and wrong eating and wrong exercise—particularly bad thinking. Do you know that many of the people who go to doctors' offices, I don't mean those who are hospitalized or who are bedridden, but many of those who are on their own two legs, and can walk down to the doctor's office, are suffering with nothing more serious than a certain $64 word called hypochondria, which means imaginary illness. Think of that. You can get mighty sick if you set your mind on the fact that you're going to be sick. Incidentally, you can be very sick, and if you make up your mind you're going to get well, the chances are that you can get well, too.

The ninth major cause of failure is unfavorable environmental influences during childhood. I have met with many a person who was a failure and never will be anything else because of certain negative influences experienced during childhood. I had a flock of those influences to overcome. I know what they can do to people. But I did have some good help in my stepmother and in Andrew Carnegie, and in the men who worked with me in building this philosophy. I had a fortunate break in life, so fortunate that I broke the grip of those negative influences that I had to meet with in my early childhood, which would have been enough to have brought me down to failure if I had not overcome them.

Number ten is lack of persistence in carrying through to a finish that which one starts. Persistence. You know, we are all good starters, but very few of us are good finishers. Do you have any idea, ladies and gentlemen, how many times the average person has to meet with failure or defeat before he quits? Do you have any idea? Well, I'd hate to give you the real statistics on it. You would be surprised but there are a great number of people who quit and accept defeat even before they start, because they lack courage and they don't ever begin anything, let alone persistently carry it through.

If you recognize the patterns of life by observing other people, you'll see that it's in the cards for everyone to meet with some defeat. The person who succeeds uses defeat, not as a stumbling block but as a stepping-stone, and rises from it with a greater urge, greater willpower, greater determination, and greater faith. Quitting, whether before or after meeting with adversity, guarantees failure.

The eleventh cause of failure is a negative mental attitude . . . a negative mental attitude. Take the average person and put any kind of a proposition before him, a new proposition, maybe one in which there exists a great opportunity for him to benefit. What is his reaction? I can tell you what it is. Immediately he begins to think about all the things in connection with it which he can't do and can't manage.

When I was offered the commission by Andrew Carnegie to become the author of the world's first philosophy of individual achievement, and was guaranteed by Mr. Carnegie that I would have the backing of the most successful men in America, to whom he would introduce me, I searched in my mind for what seemed an interminable time trying to find words with which to tell him that I didn't have the education, I didn't have the background,

I didn't have the finances to sustain myself. I could think of a dozen reasons why I couldn't accept that commission. One of the most outstanding ones was that I didn't exactly know the meaning of the word "philosophy." When I left Mr. Carnegie's study, I had to go over to the public library to look it up, to see just what it meant. That's how unprepared I was. But something inside of me said, "If Mr. Carnegie has kept you here interviewing you for three days and nights, has sold you the idea of becoming the author of this philosophy, and has promised you all of this cooperation, he must see in you something that you don't know is there. You go ahead and tell him that you can do it." And I blurted out, "Yes, Mr. Carnegie, I not only will accept the commission, but you may depend upon it, sir, that I will complete it." He said, "That's what I wanted to hear you say, and that's the tone in which I wanted to hear you say it."

I found out later on he was sitting there with a stopwatch, timing me. He was giving me sixty seconds in which to say yes or no, after I had all of the facts. I found out I had consumed exactly twenty-nine seconds; I had thirty-one seconds between me and such a destiny as no other author in my field ever, in the history of this world, has experienced. Thirty-one seconds to go, ladies and gentlemen. Because I did get my mind over on that positive side, that yes side, that can-do side, I did not let that thirty-one seconds pass by and shut me out.

Do you know there's a great river flowing in life? It's a strange river. Most people have never seen it, yet it affects their lives. Most people have been in one side or the other of it. The strangeness of this river consists in the fact that one half of it flows in one direction, and all who get into that side of it are carried to success inevitably, regardless of what they do. The other half flows in the opposite direction, and all who get in that side, just as inevitably are carried down to failure, no matter how much education they have and no matter how much effort they may put into their lives. And you say, "Fantastic. Who ever heard of a river like that?" You may not recognize it, ladies and gentlemen, but you're in that river on one side or the other right this very moment, every single solitary one of you. You're either in the negative side or you're in the positive side. One or the other, sure as you live.

And what is this river? It's not an imaginary river. It's a realistic river; it's the human mind, the power of the human mind, and you have control over it. It's the only thing in this world that you do control, or ever can control. You can switch it over to the positive side, and in a fraction of a second, you can take yourself out of the failure class into the success class, by your thinking, your mental processes, your attitude. Adversities? We all meet with adversities. But a person who has learned to negotiate this river properly and to stay in the positive side, who has learned to keep his mind positive and not negative, doesn't mind adversities. He doesn't mind defeats. He doesn't mind failures.

A person on the positive side is Marshall Field, whose successful store in Chicago burned down, and he said, "Right in that very place where those smoking embers are, I'll build the greatest store on the face of this earth." And there it stands today, ladies and gentlemen, in the Loop District of Chicago. His mental attitude was positive, in comparison with those other merchants whose stores were burned in that great Chicago fire, who said, "I'm going, we are going to move on out west. Everything's done for in Chicago." One man stood pat, grabbed the can-do side of his mental attitude, applied it to that circumstance of adversity there, and made it pay off as no other retail store has ever paid off in the world.

The twelfth major cause of failure is lack of control of the emotions of the heart. You know and I know that the emotion of love is the most precious, the most outstanding, and the most desirable thing of all, and the most dangerous. The most dangerous, underscored, exclamation point, two exclamation points. It's dangerous if you let go of both ends of the strings of your heart. If you don't have a string around your love emotions, if you let go of both ends of the strings, it's dangerous, and I do not care to whom you may release those strings. You will always run the risk of loss of control over your emotions.

I am in the business of counseling individuals and firms. I have counseled the biggest of firms. I've had the privilege of counseling two presidents of the United States, Woodrow Wilson and Franklin D. Roosevelt. I've had the privilege of counseling men who were down and out and needed a job, a place to sleep. I've had the privilege of counseling all kinds of people, and I know beyond any shadow of a doubt that if you learn to take possession of your emotions, to make the best use of them, to control them, you can rise to great heights of achievement. I also know from my observation that more people fail and fall down because of the lack of control over this emotion of love than they do because of any of the other emotions.

Thus we see that the most desirable thing in life can become the most dangerous and the most detrimental, and the greatest liability, if it is not controlled. I let loose of both ends of the string of my emotions just one time in my life, and I'm still paying for it. It cost me a million dollars right off the bat, the first year. And that was just chicken feed to what it cost me in subsequent years. I needn't go into the details; I'm afraid my wife will hear about them. Although she does know, she doesn't like to have me speak of them in public.

The number thirteen cause of failure is the desire for something for nothing, usually expressed in some form of gambling. Think of all the energy that people waste in this world trying to get something for nothing, or trying to get it for less than its value. We're living in an age now when we're seeing the great forces of our own government contributing to the downfall of people in this respect: The government knows that some people want to get something for nothing. People who want security, economic security, now look to the government for it. I'll tell you where you can get economic security: You can go out here and break into a bank, or commit a murder or something, and get into the penitentiary for life, and you needn't worry from then on out. You'll have economic security.

The only kind of economic security I want is that which I can earn with my own brain. Yet we've been educated, and we're in the process of being educated, herded, if you please, into the idea of depending upon the government for economic security. It's a false illusion. It's not going to work out.

The greatest of all privileges is the privilege of becoming self-determining, like the men who made this great country in which we live. They didn't look for economic security. Those fifty-six brave souls who signed the most marvelous document ever penned by man, the Declaration of Independence, weren't looking for economic security.

They weren't looking for bodily security. They were risking their lives because every man whose name was on that document knew that he signed what might well become his death warrant, or his license to freedom. He signed, and signed willingly. He was not looking for subsidies. He was willing to take chances, not looking for something for nothing.

I have lived, ladies and gentlemen, in the most marvelous period of this world. I have seen the death of an old age and the birth of a new one. I lived long enough in that old age to see its advantages and its disadvantages in comparison with this new and marvelous age we are living in now. I can tell you truly that anything we have that we call great in this nation, we never acquired through that tendency of people wanting to get something for nothing. That's one of the outstanding causes of failure in the lives of individuals.

Number fourteen is procrastination, the lack of the habit of reaching decisions promptly and definitely. Lack of the habit of reaching decisions promptly and definitely, especially when we have all facts in hand. People tend to put things off until tomorrow, or next week, or never. The hardest thing in the world is to get people to reach decisions. "Oh, I'll think it over," or "I'll ask my wife." When I hear a man say "I'm gonna talk it over with my wife," I know he's not going to even let his wife know anything about it. It's just an excuse for inaction, ninety-nine times out of a hundred.

The number fifteen cause of failure is giving in to one or more of the seven basic fears. I wonder if you know what the seven basic fears are? The first one is the fear of poverty. Why a person in a great country like this, where opportunity is abundant for every living being, should be afraid of poverty, I don't know. But I do know that the vast majority of people are afraid they'll lose what they have. Afraid they'll lose their job; afraid they'll lose their home. Afraid of this, afraid of that, afraid of the other thing.

Number two of the seven basic fears is the fear of criticism. Isn't that an astounding thing, how that'll slow men down? Afraid of what "they" will say. I have heard people talk about "they" a long time; I have never seen "they" in person. I don't know who "they" are. But there are millions of people who stand in mortal fear of what somebody will say if they step out of line, one step away from the beaten path, and do something in a new way. Henry Ford wasn't afraid of criticism, and he got plenty of it when he put out that horseless carriage. As a matter of fact, they threatened to have him arrested if he brought it onto the streets of Detroit. He had to get a special permit to operate it. He wouldn't be stopped just because people criticized him.

I can remember when I was first building this philosophy. People criticized me and said, "Napoleon Hill thinks he is building the world's first philosophy of success, and he himself doesn't have two nickels to rub together." The unfortunate part of it, ladies and gentlemen, was they were telling the truth. I didn't have two nickels, but I have two nickels now. I have a lot of other things economically and financially and otherwise now that the majority of people never do acquire in life, because I not only acquired these principles, but I put them to use in my own life. I not only teach them, but I live them. And they have brought me the blessings of life that the majority of people want but never get.

The third basic fear is the fear of ill health, the fourth is the fear of loss of love, the fifth is the fear of old age, the sixth is the fear of the loss of liberty, and the seventh is the fear of death.

Ladies and gentlemen, if you want the real causes of failure, there they are, done up in a package that you can understand. Remember that crooked river I mentioned before, crooked because it followed the path of least resistance? So many of these fifteen major causes of failure, such as drifting, lack of a definite major purpose, inadequate education, lack of self-discipline, lack of ambition, lack of persistence, the desire for something for nothing, and failure to make decisions, are caused by taking this path.

The successful man always fights hard to do the right thing, and never chooses the path of least resistance. All rivers do choose this path, but successful men never do.

Please join me next time when I will focus on how to overcome these causes of failure. And I thank you.

8

PERSISTENCE AND DECISIVENESS

Hello, ladies and gentlemen. I am Henry Alderburg, the associate director of education of the Napoleon Hill Institute. Mr. Hill has invited me here to meet the people of Paris, which I enjoyed doing this week, and I will be conducting our discussion today with Mr. Hill. Mr. Hill in previous broadcasts has presented the success formula which people can live by at their work and play, in their jobs and home. While you have been telling our audience what they must do in order to achieve success, Mr. Hill, you also told our friends what they must not do, detailing in the last broadcast the fifteen major causes of failure. Will you continue your discussion of the causes of failure today, and of how to overcome them?

Mr. Hill: Yes, we will begin our program today by describing the two most common causes of failure. You will observe that these stumbling blocks can be converted into stepping-stones to success by the simple process of following the rules I have previously presented. After discussing these causes and how to overcome them through persistence and decisiveness, I will tell our audience how failure can be converted into success.

Cause of failure number one is the habit of quitting when the going is hard. No matter who you are or how skilled you may be in your occupation, there will be times when the going is hard and unpleasant circumstances will overtake you. If you yield easily to these obstacles you may as well write yourself off as far as becoming a great success is concerned. But, assuming that you will follow the success rules I have presented in these programs, when you meet with opposition of any nature, instead of quitting you will turn on more willpower, stoke the fires of a stronger faith in your own ability, and make up your mind that come what may you will not sell yourself short. Do that and you will soon succeed.

I had one of the greatest insights of my life when Thomas A. Edison told me how he reacted to failure when he was trying to perfect the incandescent electric lamp. Before he found the solution to his problem he tried more than ten thousand different ideas, every one of which was a failure. Just think of that, a man keeping on despite ten thousand failures with faith unshaken, and at long last being crowned with victory. One failure is sufficient to make the average person quit. Perhaps this is why there are so many average persons and there was only one Thomas A. Edison.

Cause of failure number two is procrastination, the inability to make prompt and definite decisions. Procrastination is the habit of waiting for something beneficial to happen instead of getting busy and making something happen. All successful people make it their habit to create circumstances and opportunities favorable to themselves instead of accepting whatever life offers them.

Mr. Alderburg: Could you tell us what happens to the person who fails to move on his own to achieve and embrace opportunity when it presents itself?

Mr. Hill: Yes, I can give you a wonderful illustration of the cost of this indecision and procrastination. Some years ago one of the large automobile manufacturing companies decided to begin an extensive expansion program. The president called in one hundred young men from the various departments of the plant and said to them: "Gentlemen, we are going to enlarge our plant and greatly increase our output of automobiles, which means that we will need executives and department managers far beyond our present staff. We are offering each of you young men the privilege of working four hours per day in the office, where you will learn to become executives, and four hours at your regular jobs in the plant. There will be some home-work you must do at night and there may be times when you will have to forgo your social duties and work over-time. Your pay will be the same that you are now getting in the plant. I am passing out cards on which I wish each of you who will accept our offer to write your name, and I will give you one hour in which to talk among yourselves and make up your minds."

Mr. Alderburg: Of course all of them accepted the opportunity?

Mr. Hill: No, they didn't. When the president of the company picked up the cards, he got one of the biggest surprises of his life. Only twenty-three out of the one hun-dred had accepted the offer. The next day thirty more of the men came into the president's office and informed him they had made up their minds to accept, some of them ex-plaining they had reached the decision to accept after talking the matter over with their wives.

Mr. Alderburg: What happened to the thirty that did that?

Mr. Hill: The president said: "Gentlemen, you were given one hour in which to make up your minds after you had all of the facts concerning my offer that I could give you. I am very, very sorry but this opportunity is gone for-ever, because I have learned from experience that the man who cannot or will not make up his mind quickly and definitely when he has all of the necessary facts to enable him to do so, will change his mind quickly at the first sign of obstacles, or he will allow other people to talk him into changing his mind."

Mr. Alderburg: Mr. Hill, you have told a remarkable story and it is somewhat similar to your relationship with Andrew Carnegie, which shows what promptness of decision can do to help one seize upon a favorable opportunity. I am sure our audience would like you to describe your experience, which was destined to benefit not only yourself but millions of men and women throughout the world.

Mr. Hill: The experience you mentioned happened over forty years ago when I first met Andrew Carnegie, the great industrialist who founded the United States Steel Corporation. I described it briefly in our last broadcast. I went to see Mr. Carnegie to write a success story for Bob Taylor's magazine based on his stupendous achievements. Originally he allotted me three hours for the interview, but actually it lasted three days and nights during which he was also interviewing me with a purpose in mind, without my knowing what he was up to. During those three days he was telling me that the world needed a new success philosophy, one that would give the average man or woman the full benefit of all that he and other successful men like himself had learned from a lifetime of experience.

Mr. Carnegie said it was a sin of major proportions that successful men allowed their hard-earned experience to be buried with their bones.

At the end of the third day, Mr. Carnegie said: "I have been talking to you for three days about the need for a written success philosophy. I am going to ask you one question which I want you to answer with a simple yes or no, but don't answer it until you make up your mind definitely. If I commission you to organize the world's first practical success philosophy, will you devote twenty years to research and to interviewing successful people, and earn your own way without a financial subsidy from me, yes or no?"

Mr. Alderburg: Of course you told him yes, because if you hadn't done so we wouldn't be here on this program today, would we?

Mr. Hill: I said, "Yes, Mr. Carnegie, I'll accept your offer and you may depend upon it, sir, that I will carry it out to the finish." Mr. Carnegie said, "All right, you have the job and I like the mental attitude in which you accepted the assignment." I learned some years later that Mr. Carnegie was holding a stopwatch under his desk, and in his mind he had given me exactly sixty seconds in which to make up my mind, after he had given me three whole days in which to get the facts.

Mr. Alderburg: Why do you suppose Mr. Carnegie

placed so much emphasis on the matter of prompt deci-sion?

Mr. Hill: He explained that no one can be counted upon to carry out important assignments or to assume important responsibilities without following the habit of quick and definite decisions. Mr. Carnegie was also search-ing for another quality without which he knew I would never follow through with twenty years of research, which quality was necessary in order to find out what makes successful men and women.

Mr. Alderburg: What quality was that?

Mr. Hill: It was the habit of turning on more willpower instead of quitting when the going is hard. Mr. Carnegie knew that there is always a time in every undertaking when one meets with obstacles and is overtaken by opposition, and he recognized that the quitter never wins and the win-ner never quits.

Mr. Alderburg: What was your greatest obstacle that you had to overcome while you were doing the twenty years of research in organizing the success philosophy which has made you famous throughout the world?

Mr. Hill: You are going to be surprised. My greatest obstacle was friends and relatives who believed I had undertaken too big a job. They chided me for working for the richest man in the world for twenty years without financial compensation from him. One of the queer traits of most people, especially one's own relatives, is that they so often discourage any member of the family who steps out ahead of the crowd and aspires to achieve outstanding success.

Mr. Alderburg: How did you manage to keep up your spirits and sustain your faith for so long a time, in the face of this opposition from your relatives?

Mr. Hill: I didn't do it alone. I had help through a mastermind alliance with two people who gave me encouragement when the going was tough. These were Mr. Carnegie, my sponsor, and my stepmother, who was the only member of my family that believed I would endure through twenty years of rough going. One of the great miracles in human relations consists in the power of survival, which one may acquire by a friendly alliance with one or more other persons.

Mr. Alderburg: Did you get help from other successful men besides Mr. Carnegie while you were organizing the philosophy of success?

Mr. Hill: Oh, yes, and if I hadn't we wouldn't be here on this program today. There was scarcely a single person of outstanding achievements during my association with Mr. Carnegie who didn't cooperate with me by supplying a portion of that which went into the making of the science of success. But I also learned one interesting fact about many people while I was struggling to complete my work and receive recognition. I learned that when one needs anything very badly, it is very difficult for him to find anyone who wishes to help him get it, but when one gets over the hump, achieves recognition, and no longer needs help, then just about everybody on earth wants to do something for him.

Mr. Alderburg: Isn't there something in the Bible that corroborates what you just said?

Mr. Hill: Yes, there is, and while I am not going to try to undertake to quote it verbatim, it goes something like this: To him that hath, it shall be given, and to him that hath not, it shall be taken away even unto that which he has. The first time I read this passage in the Bible I questioned the soundness of it, but the sober experience of later years proves conclusively that this is a trait of mankind. No one wants to be associated with or to help a failure, while almost everyone will go out of their way to help one who doesn't need help. This is explained by the law through which like attracts like.

Let me call your attention to the fact that every failure, every adversity, and every unpleasant circumstance carries with it the seed of an equivalent benefit or advantage, and the person who has a sound philosophy to live by learns very quickly how to find this seed of equivalent benefit and to germinate it into advantage. As far as luck is concerned, it may be true that it often does play a temporary part in the lives of people, but remember this: If luck brings temporary defeat or failure, one doesn't have to accept this as permanent, and by searching for that seed of equivalent benefit, one may actually transform a failure into an enduring success.

Mr. Alderburg: Could you give me an example illustrating your point that adversity carries with it the seed of an equivalent benefit?

Mr. Hill: Yes, there are hundreds of examples I could provide, if time permitted, but I'll give you two, one of which changed the entire course of my life, and through my efforts it has changed the lives of many people. My mother passed away when I was only eight years old. To most people that of course would seem like a terrible loss, but the seed of an equivalent benefit which came from my loss was found in a wise and understanding stepmother who took my mother's place and inspired me with courage and faith when I most needed it.

The other example is that of Abraham Lincoln's great sorrow over the loss of his first love, the death of Ann Rutledge. That experience reached deeply into the spiritual forces of the great Lincoln's soul and revealed to the world the qualities which were destined to make him one of the greatest presidents in the time of our greatest need. You might say it was bad luck or misfortune which deprived Lincoln of his first love, but it was Lincoln's reaction and adjustment to this loss which revealed the greatness of his soul. He responded by recommitting himself to his professional and personal ambitions, and reaching for the stars. No human experience should ever be charged off as a complete loss, because every circumstance of our lives, whether pleasant or unpleasant, places us in the way of learning how to live and how to get along with other people.

Mr. Alderburg: Speaking of adversity, during your contacts with Mr. Edison, did you get the impression that he was handicapped by his deafness?

Mr. Hill: No, on the contrary. Much to my surprise, I discovered that Mr. Edison's deafness was a blessing instead of a curse because he found the seed of an equivalent benefit that his deafness yielded, and he made astounding use of that seed. Once I asked Mr. Edison if his deafness were not a handicap and he said, "No, it is a blessing instead because it has taught me to hear from within."

Mr. Alderburg: Just what did Mr. Edison mean by that remark?

Mr. Hill: He meant that his deafness had caused him to tune in and make stronger contact with sources of knowledge outside of those available through the capacity of hearing. It was from these sources that he got much of the knowledge which made him the greatest inventor of all time. While I'm on this subject, may I tell you that throughout the twenty years I spent analyzing successful people to learn what made them tick, I discovered that successful people almost invariably were successful in exact proportion to the extent that they had met and overcome obstacles and defeat.

Mr. Alderburg: How do you explain this?

Mr. Hill: It can be explained by considering that nature has so arranged the affairs of men that strength grows out of struggle. If men had no problems and were never forced to exert themselves, they would atrophy and wither away through disuse of their brain cells, the same as would happen with an arm or leg if it were not given exercise. Nature penalizes people for neglecting to properly use their physical bodies, as everyone knows, and the same is true of their brain cells with which they think. If we do not use the mind it becomes lazy and unreliable. Human problems force people to develop their minds through use.

Look what happens to the children of very wealthy people, who allow their offspring to grow up under the delusion that because their parents have money, they don't have to work or to prepare themselves to live on their own initiative. Very rarely does such a person become fully independent or self-determining.

Mr. Alderburg: You had some experiences with struggle during your early days, didn't you?

Mr. Hill: Yes, I was blessed at birth with four powerful causes for struggle, namely, poverty, fear, superstition, and illiteracy.

Mr. Alderburg: Did you say blessings?

Mr. Hill: Yes, blessings, because I was destined to devote my life to helping my fellow men overcome these four common causes of failure, and I needed to learn something about them at their source. On the lighter side of my blessings, you may be interested in knowing that I was tagged with the name Napoleon with the hope of my parents that a great uncle by the same name would leave me a portion of his fortune when he died. Fortunately he didn't. I say fortunately because I know what happened to those to whom he did leave his money. Whereas I, in my struggle to master poverty, fear, superstition, and illiteracy, uncovered knowledge which I have been privileged to share with millions of people who have benefited by it; they received only money, which did not last long.

Mr. Alderburg: If you had a friend or a son or a listener who was preparing to make his own way in the world, and you had to select one trait on which you would urge him to depend mostly for success, what would this trait be?

Mr. Hill: That's a $64 question, but without hesitation I'll say that I would select that trait which inspires or compels a person to keep on going when the going is hard instead of giving up and quitting. I would select this trait because it is the one which has served me at times when my future seemed hopeless better than any other trait, by any standard of evaluation, and I would select it because I have never seen or heard of anyone who achieved success above mediocrity without it. And I would select it because I have reason to believe that the Creator intended people to become wise and strong through struggle.

Mr. Alderburg: Your remarks about the sons of very rich men prompts me to ask if during your contact with wealthy Americans you discovered any son of a rich man who equaled or excelled his father in business or otherwise?

Mr. Hill: Only one, and that was John D. Rockefeller Jr., who not only caught up with the achievements of his father, but to my way of thinking excelled his father in many respects. Inherited wealth is almost always a great curse. Poverty is often a great curse as well, but only because people accept it as such and not as an inspiration to render the sort of service which can overcome poverty.

Mr. Alderburg: From what you've been saying, I judge that you believe a poor man's son has a much better chance of success than the son of a rich man.

Mr. Hill: All of my observations during the past forty-odd years convince me conclusively that the poor man's son has a better chance provided that he does not accept poverty as something he has to tolerate, and makes up his mind to master it.

Mr. Alderburg: What was your first reaction to Andrew Carnegie's offer to you to sponsor you to write a philosophy of success on condition that you earn your own way, without a cash subsidy from him?

Mr. Hill: My first reaction was the same as that which most anyone would have experienced. I believed that his requirements were unfair in view of his great wealth. But I learned later that this was one of the shrewdest moves that Mr. Carnegie ever made in his relations with me, because he forced me to become resourceful and to learn how to apply the principles of success in sustaining myself while engaged in the then unprofitable work of research into the causes of success. Because of this foresight on the part of Mr. Carnegie, I lived to see the day, and it was not too far off from my beginning with him, when I didn't need financial help.

Mr. Alderburg: I suppose that many of our friends would be interested in knowing how you managed to support yourself during the twenty years of research you devoted to your work before it became profitable.

Mr. Hill: I have been asked that same question many times. I was an experienced newspaperman when I first met Mr. Carnegie, and my work in this field sustained me for a time. Later I began to train men and women in salesmanship, and it turned out that I had talent in this field. During my work in the field of salesmanship I trained over thirty thousand people, many of whom became outstanding master salesmen.

Mr. Alderburg: Just one more personal question and I'll let you off the hook. How do you manage to stay so energetic and active and young at the age of sixty-five?

Mr. Hill: Thank you. I remain young by keeping busy in a labor of love and by the habit of celebrating every birthday by taking off a year from my age instead of adding one. I am now back in my late thirties. But, perhaps to speak more seriously, I close each day's labor with a prayer, which keeps my store of blessings eternally filled, and I shall express that prayer now: Oh Infinite Intelligence, I ask not for more riches but for more wisdom with which to make better use of the blessings with which I was endowed at birth to reach the goal of embracing my own mind and directing it to ends of my own choice. Amen.

Mr. Alderburg: Mr. Hill, the time has come now for you to answer a few of the many questions that have come into our office in reference to problems that have arisen in the minds of individuals. Will you give our listeners the benefit of your wise counsel in answering some of them? The first one comes from a woman who says: "I'm secretary to a man who believes that a woman is not entitled to promotion to an executive job. I have the ability to fill a more responsible position. How should I go about getting that position?"

Mr. Hill: I would suggest that you manage to get permission to do some of the work connected with the higher position, and that you do it on your own time and without compensation. It is not likely that your employer would object to your working overtime without pay, and by doing so you will prove your ability to fill the better position.

Mr. Alderburg: The next one comes from a man who desires to go into business for himself. He says: "I work for a large trucking company and I know their business from top to bottom. I wish to start a trucking business of my own but I do not have the capital with which to buy the necessary equipment. How do you suggest that I get the necessary money?"

Mr. Hill: First you should advertise for a partner who would be willing to lend you the necessary capital and who would also take over a portion of the responsibilities of the business. In this way you would match your experience with the other fellow's money, and the arrangement should be satisfactory to both of you if you get the right man. Try an advertisement in the financial section of the local newspaper and the *Wall Street Journal* and you will likely find the man you need.

Mr. Alderburg: Here's one from a young man who's

about to finish high school. He says: "I will be graduating this year and I wish to get a position with some able businessman so I may get the benefit of his experience. What should I do to get such a position?"

Mr. Hill: One approach would be for you to take a business college training course, unless you can get the business training in the high school, and prepare yourself as a secretary. Good secretaries are exceedingly hard to find, and you would have no trouble locating a position. You could practically be sure of choosing your own employer. In a job of this sort you would have access to business contacts and the benefits of the experiences of successful businessmen, which would be of priceless value to you as a stepping-stone to something better.

Mr. Alderburg: Here is a question from a housewife who writes: "Would you please tell me how I can find some sort of work I can do at home to add to our family income. Before I was married I was chief operator for a telephone company and I have a very pleasing telephone voice."

Mr. Hill: You can capitalize on your telephone experience and your pleasing voice by selling merchandise over the telephone, or by procuring qualified leads for life insurance men, automobile salesmen, or practically any other source of services or merchandise. You would have but little difficulty in reaching the heads of families by telephone through the wires. I know one woman who has a battery of more than a dozen telephones working in New York City. She has a staff of trained operators to assist her, and she is making more money than the average business-man earns.

Mr. Alderburg: A college professor says: "A growing family makes it necessary for me to earn more money than my present position as a teacher now pays. What should I do about this?"

Mr. Hill: The answer to that is obvious. Get into some other field of endeavor such as selling, for example. You could make the break from your present work by starting as a part-time salesman working during evenings until you prove to yourself that you can sell.

Mr. Alderburg: Thank you, Mr. Hill, for your counsel to these problems. We have run out of broadcast time. Ladies and gentlemen, join us next time when Napoleon Hill will further detail the Principles of Success his years of research have discovered.

Mr. Hill: Thank you, everyone. I hope you learned today how decisiveness and persistence can help you turn adversity into advantage and overcome the causes of fail-ure. Next time I will discuss self-discipline, another criti-cal success principle.

9

SELF-DISCIPLINE

Good evening, ladies and gentlemen, and welcome to another broadcast about the essential principles of the science of success. Tonight's subject is self-discipline. I think, perhaps, if there is one thing that people need more than all other things combined, it is discipline over self. How little attention most of us give to that great subject.

I want to tell you something: I want to suggest to you in the beginning of this broadcast that in order to make the greatest use of self-discipline, you've got to have a system to go by. You've got to have a plan. You've got to keep your mind occupied at all times with all the things and all the circumstances and all the desires of your choice, and strictly off of the things that you don't want.

Here is self-discipline in its highest order: keeping your mind fixed on the things you do want in life, and off the things you don't want. Do you know that the majority of people go all the way through life with their minds dominated by the things that they don't want? Fear of ill health, fear of poverty, and fear of criticism. If you want to know the grandfather of all the fears, it's the fear of criticism. I think back in the early days, when I was first starting my research, that was my most difficult stumbling block. I was afraid of what "they" would say. I never did find out just who "they" were, but I certainly was afraid of them.

My method of exercising self-discipline consists in what I call the eight princes, the eight imaginary beings which I have created and associated with my inner ego, whose duty it is to supply me with everything that I need to be happy and successful and prosperous and healthful. I would recommend that technique to you, but if you prefer some other technique, perhaps your idea would work just as well.

Your reward for taking possession of your own mind and keeping it fixed on the things that you want consists in mastery of your own destiny through the guidance of infinite intelligence. And, I should say, that should be quite reward enough. The one thing that the Creator intended every human being to do was to exercise complete control over his own mind, and to direct that mind to the attainment of whatever the individual considered to be necessary for his success and peace of mind. We sometimes take that great prerogative—and it is the greatest thing in the world, undoubtedly—we take that and we direct it not to the attainment of the things we want, but to the attainment of the things we don't want.

The penalty for not taking possession of your own mind, not disciplining it, consists in the fact that you will become the victim of the stray winds of circumstance, which will remain forever beyond your control. In other words, you'll be blown hither and yon in life, just like the dry leaf on the wind, if you don't learn to take possession of your own mind, and to keep it focused on things that are beneficial to you, and off things that are not beneficial.

You may be interested in knowing that while I was building the science of success, I also had to rebuild Napoleon Hill. It was a terrific job, because I almost had to start from scratch—maybe below scratch; at least I did a lot of scratching. At thirteen different points I had to rebuild my own character through self-discipline. I want you to observe carefully these thirteen points, and as I go along, compare them with yourself and see wherein you might benefit by exercising self-discipline as I had to exercise it, as I went along.

First of all, back in the early days I didn't have self-confidence. You wouldn't believe it, perhaps, to know me now, but I didn't. I believed in about everything else except

Napoleon Hill. I used to think that if I could only get the cooperation of Henry Ford and Thomas Edison, and other men of that kind, their personal cooperation, that I could then attain great things, that I perhaps could achieve success as important as theirs. I courted that co-operation, and craved it, only to learn later on that I didn't need it. I learned that I could do the job by myself, if I believed enough in myself.

Second, I had to gain discipline over myself in master-ing the seven basic fears, and especially the fear of poverty and the fear of criticism. I want to tell you, those were two great stumbling blocks. I didn't get very far in life until I learned to overcome them. When anybody criticizes me now, I don't get mad about it, as I used to do, but I begin to examine myself. I first of all examine the person doing the criticizing, to see if he's capable of making an intelli-gent criticism. If he is, I then examine myself very care-fully, to see if the criticism is worthy, and very often I discover that it is. By observing the benefits of criticism from others, I have learned to improve myself from year to year.

Third, I had to use self-discipline in removing my self-imposed limitations. It would be interesting, my friends, if you would sit down one of these days and take inventory, and put it on paper, of the places and the circumstances where you limit yourself—starting, for instance, with your income. People in certain income brackets stay there practically all the way through their lives, mainly because they don't raise those limits and aim for something bigger. In a great country like this, where opportunities are abundant, there is no reason for anybody limiting himself as to his income.

Fourth, I had to use self-discipline in recognizing and embracing my prerogative power to use my own mind, and to direct it to whatever ends I chose. I venture the suggestion that there's not a person in this audience who hasn't made that same mistake of not embracing this power, and who doesn't need now to begin exercising discipline over the mind, to the extent that you'll take possession of it and you'll direct it to the things you want in life, and not allow it to drift through the circumstances that you don't want.

I had to discipline myself on that point for a number of years, and I wonder how you stand on that subject now. I am not going to ask you to raise your hands, nor to vote, nor to let me know. I am going to ask you to think about it in your own hearts and minds: the extent to which you are exercising control over your own minds.

Fifth, I had to use self-discipline over a long period of years to relate myself to fame and material riches in a spirit of humble gratitude. If you work hard enough and if you work intelligently, and if you use this philosophy and apply it, the day may well come when you'll be both famous and perhaps richer than you need to be. That is where and when you will need to watch yourself very carefully, because if you attain fame and fortune, and do not attain gratitude along with it, the chances are that you will not enjoy that fame or that fortune.

There was a time when I would have given a king's ransom to have had the recognition and the fame that I have today. But if I'd had it then, I probably wouldn't have been as grateful as I am today, because I can assure you that the road through which I attained it has been a long and a hard one.

Sixth, I had to use self-discipline to sow the seeds of service before trying to harvest a crop of reward. I rather suspect that most of you will need to observe this point very carefully. The majority of people in the world need to discipline themselves by recognizing that before you can harvest, you have first got to sow. The majority of people in the world today are trying to reap before they sow. That is to say, they are trying to get something for nothing, or trying to get something for less than its value, trying to find a bargain at life's marketplace. I can tell you frankly that life has no bargains. Everything that you get that's worthy of having has a price upon it. If you don't pay that price, you don't get that thing; you get some substitute— something that looks like it but isn't as good.

Seventh, I had to use self-discipline in that I used to give away ninety percent of my time, and sell ten percent of it. I want to tell you that those odds were wrong. There are a lot of people today whom I know who are not doing so well in life because they give away too much of their service. I advocate in this philosophy going the extra mile, doing more than you're paid for, yes. But I also advocate that after you have gone the extra mile and have rendered useful service, you should see to it that life pays off in one form or another, that you don't neglect yourself. I think perhaps the selling of ninety percent of your time, and the giving away of ten percent, is about the right amount.

Number eight, I had to use self-discipline in connection with the false belief that honesty and sincerity of purpose are sufficient for success. If you believe that, my friends, perish the idea. Honesty and sincerity of purpose are very desirable traits of virtue, of course, but they are not enough to ensure success. You've got to have other things to go along with them. To be exact, you have to have everything that's represented by the seventeen principles of success before you can be sure of success in this world. At the very least, you have to apply some combination of those seventeen principles.

I made a survey of the state-run homes for the poor in Virginia back some years ago, and I found out that nearly all the people in those public houses, being cared for by the state, were there because they were honest, sure they were, but they didn't look out for their own interests, nor their own rights. They had to have something besides honesty to succeed.

Ninth, I had to use self-discipline in connection with my failure to budget and use my time more beneficially. I'm not going to ask you to raise your hands and let me know how many of you have a time budget by which to work, but I'm going to suggest to you that you think about the importance of having that. If you don't have one, get one. Lay out your time so that there's a certain portion of it that you devote to each of the necessary things that you want to accomplish in life. Don't let anything interfere with that budget.

Ten, I had to use self-discipline to stick to my major purpose in life, especially for the first twenty years after I began my success research. There were times when I had attractive commercial offers made to me to use my talents and ability to make money and to get away from the creation of this philosophy. Every time that I nearly gave way to the temptation to go off on a tangent, I was able to stay on track. Sticking to your definite major purpose for twenty years when it's not paying off in dollars and cents is not an easy job, and I want to tell you that you've got to have a lot of self-discipline if you're going to go through with it.

Eleven, I needed self-discipline due to lack of patience. I didn't have an awful lot of patience in the beginning. I don't know whether I have too much now or not, or whether I have enough. But I can tell you one thing: I have a lot more than I used to have. If you're going to be happy and have peace of mind, and get along in harmony with people in this chaotic world, you've got to have a lot of patience. You've got to have a lot of patience with the things that are happening in the high offices of the United States today as well. Every day, every day something's happening to try the patience of the citizens. We've got to be patient.

Number twelve, I had to use self-discipline to correct my failure to inventory and express gratitude for my intangible riches. I wonder how many of you have done that, ever, in your lives—have made an inventory of your intangible riches. I'm not talking about the kind of riches that you can place in the bank. I had, during my research in building the science of success, the collaboration of more men, more intelligent and successful men, than has ever been back of any one philosopher or author or lecturer in the history of this world, as far as I know. For a long time, at least the first twenty or twenty-five years of my adult life, I didn't fully appreciate the wonderful opportunity that I'd had, and I didn't include in my category of riches the marvelous benefits of the experiences that I got from those men who helped me. In other words, I hadn't developed a keen sense of gratitude.

I think, my friends, that if you don't have a keen sense of gratitude for the blessings that you enjoy, and if you don't have a keen sense of loyalty to those to whom you owe loyalty, you are poor, no matter what else you may have in life.

Thirteenth, and last, I had to use self-discipline in controlling my ambition to demonstrate opulence. It took two large estates, one in the Catskill Mountains and one in Florida, and two Rolls-Royce automobiles at $22,500 each, to teach me the virtues of the simple style of living. That's quite a confession for me to have to make, but I might as well let you know now that I've made some mistakes, too. I suspect you would have a hard time finding anyone anywhere who lives a more simple life than Mrs. Hill and I do today. And we're enjoying ourselves. We have freedom, we have peace of mind, we have health, we have everything that we need or want or can use.

I used to load myself down with a lot of things that I didn't use. I thought it was necessary to set up a front, to demonstrate to the world that I not only taught the rules of success, but that I could demonstrate them. I don't look at the matter that way now. Through self-discipline I have learned to be myself under all circumstances. I say what I think and think what I say. If I want to drive an old, inexpensive car, I can do it; I don't have to have a new Rolls-Royce. If I want to appear in a public place in a business suit instead of a dress suit or a tuxedo, which I do quite often—as a matter of fact, I don't own a tuxedo or a dress suit anymore—I can do it. I've disciplined myself to be myself, to be Napoleon Hill, not to try to ape or to imitate anyone, for any purpose. It's going to take a lot of self-discipline for you to get in that frame of mind.

Listening to these thirteen points, you learn the importance of self-discipline. Without it, one just drifts through life. Without it, one follows the path of least resistance, as do all rivers to their benefit—and, unfortunately, some men to their certain detriment.

I want to emphasize the necessity for disciplining oneself in connection with one particular subject, and that subject is the use of time. Time is the great universal doctor of human ills, whose chief agent is the energy which connects everything with every other thing in the universe. We must use self-discipline to control our use of time.

Time is the great healer of wounds, both physical and mental. It is the transformer of all causes into their appropriate effects. There are some things that we consider ills and discomforts and disadvantages and adversities, ladies and gentlemen, which can only be cured with time. Nothing else can do it. You've got to learn to time your adversities and your disappointments. You've got to learn to time everything. Time trades irrational youth for the maturity of age and wisdom. Isn't that a marvelous thing, to know that time trades the mistakes of youth for the wisdom of age? When you hear a person complaining about becoming old, you ought to break the news to him that if he's attaining along with his age the proper amount of wisdom, as nature intended, that it's a great blessing.

Time can change the wounds of the heart and the frustrations of our daily lives into courage, endurance, and understanding. Without this kindly and beneficent service, most individuals would be lost in the early days of their youth. How absolutely true that is. If you look back into the days of your youth, you can see that if you hadn't had time on your side you really would have been hurt. Time ripens the grain in the fields and the fruit on the trees, and makes them ready for human enjoyment and sustenance. Time gives hotheads a chance to cool off—now isn't that a humdinger? I think that fact should be emphasized. Who of us has not been so unfortunate as to have needed some cooling off?

Time helps us to discover the great laws of nature by the trial-and-error method, and to profit by our mistakes of judgment. Time is our most precious possession, because we can be sure of no more of it than a single second at any one time. That's all you're sure of, one second at a time.

Time is the agent of mercy, through which we may repent of our sins and errors, and gain useful knowledge therefrom. You can actually transform your sins and mistakes into advantages, but you can do it only through time.

Time favors those who interpret nature's laws correctly, and who adapt them as guideposts in the correct habits of living. But time swings heavily with penalties for those who ignore or neglect these laws. Time is the master manipulator of the universal law of cosmic habit force, the fixer of all habits, both of living creatures and of inanimate things. Time is also the master manipulator of the law of compensation, through the operation of which everyone reaps that which he sows. Time does not always operate the law of compensation swiftly, but it does operate it definitely, according to fixed habits and patterns which the philosopher understands, and by which he can foretell the nature of coming events by examining the cause from which they had to spring.

Time is also the master manipulator of the great law of change, which keeps all things and people in a constant state of flux, and never allows them to remain the same for two minutes in succession. This truth is laden with benefits of stupendous proportions, because it provides the means by which we may correct our mistakes and eliminate our false fears and weak habits. Go back to your past experiences and take count of the occasions when your troubled heart found no surcease from its aches and pains save only by the merciful hand of Dr. Time.

Here is a summary of an essay which I wrote, entitled "My Commitment to Dr. Time." Number one, time is my greatest asset, and I shall relate myself to it on a budget system which provides that every second not devoted to sleep shall be used for self-improvement in one way or another. Two, in the future I shall regard the loss through neglect of any portion of my time as a sin for which I must atone so that I can make better use in the future of an equivalent amount of time. I do waste some time, but I usually try to make up for it later on, by making better use of my time. Three, recognizing that I shall reap that which I sow, I shall sow only the seeds of service which may benefit others as well as myself, and thereby throw myself in the way of the great law of compensation, and benefit from it. Four, I shall so use my time in the future that each day brings me a greater measure of peace of mind, in the absence of which I shall recognize that the seed I have been sowing needs reexamination.

Five, knowing that my habits of thought become the patterns which attract all circumstances affecting my life through the lapse of time, I will keep my mind so busy in connection with the circumstances I desire that no time will be left to devote to the fears and the frustrations, and the other things I do not desire. I think perhaps that's the greatest plank in the platform.

Next, recognizing that, at best, my allotted time on earth is indefinite and limited, I shall endeavor in all ways possible to use my portion of it so that those nearest me will benefit by my influence, and be inspired by my example to make the best possible use of their own time. Last, I will repeat this commitment daily during the remainder of my allotment of life, and back it with the belief that it will improve my character and inspire those whom I may influence to likewise improve their lives.

So you can see that time can do wondrous things. But it can also slip away. It takes vigilant application of self-discipline to make time work to your benefit.

Thank you for listening, ladies and gentlemen. Please join me next week when I will bring you the first of two programs on the importance of developing a pleasing personality to achieving success.

10

PLEASING PERSONALITY

Good evening, ladies and gentlemen. Our subject tonight and next week is the importance of a pleasing personality. There are three important points at which people contact you and evaluate your personality, whether you recognize it or not. First, they evaluate you according to how you look to them when they first look you over. Someone has said that clothes make the man. I don't know whether that's true or not. I doubt, strictly speaking, that it is true, but I do know one thing: Clothes certainly do go a long way to introducing the man properly on first acquaintanceship. There's no doubt about that. And there is only one chance to make a first impression.

The second point of contact from which people evaluate your personality is according to how your voice registers with them. Do you know that we often judge others based not on their words so much as their tone of voice? I don't believe that you need to be an expert in psychology or in anything else to recognize, when you hear a person talking, whether that person is sincere or not. I know that you don't have much confidence in a person unless there is sincerity in back of what he's saying.

The third point of contact from which people evaluate your personality is according to how they feel when they're near you. I mean, how they feel without your saying anything or without your doing anything. Whether you know it or not, you're definitely communicating your mental attitude toward other people without opening your mouth, without saying anything at all.

Speaking of this business of personality, a friend of mine had a wife whom he said he didn't take out with him as much as she wanted to go because her personality never attracted anybody. In other words, she was never an asset to him, but always a liability. She didn't like her husband's statement; she said, "I'll bet you anything you want to bet that if you walk down the street with me, just get behind me where you can watch me, that every person that passes me will turn and look at me when I go by." The husband said, "I'll just take you up on that." Well, they started down the street, and sure enough, the men in particular turned and gazed at her, every single solitary one of them. Women did, too, and sometimes the women turned up their noses a little bit. But nevertheless, they did turn around and look. What the husband didn't know, walking behind her, was that as she passed each one of these people, she made an ugly face at them. Naturally, they turned around and looked, in surprise and puzzlement.

One of the important things that is responsible for your success or your failure is your personality, which consists of some twenty-five major factors. The object of these broadcasts tonight and next week is to give you a chance to take down a list of these twenty-five factors, which I hope you will do, and sometime very soon rate yourself on each of them. The rating should be good, fair, and poor. I am going to give them to you slowly enough and clearly enough that you can write them down. The analysis will be far more beneficial to you if, after you have rated yourself on these twenty-five factors of a pleasing personality, you turn the list over to someone who knows you real well, maybe your wife or your husband, and let that person give you a second rating. You may be surprised at the difference in the ratings on some of these points.

Your personality consists in the sum total of your mental and physical traits which distinguish you from all other people. It is the factor which, more than all others, determines whether you are liked or disliked. It is the medium through which you negotiate your way through life, and it determines very largely your ability to deal with others with a minimum amount of friction.

The financial value of personality may be reckoned by observing that those who have a negative personality seldom are found in positions in the higher brackets of income, while those with a pleasing personality have little difficulty in selling themselves successfully in all human relationships, in social and domestic relationships no less than in the office and the shop. Andrew Carnegie, my sponsor, the great philanthropist and industrialist, once said that he paid Charles M. Schwab $75,000 a year as president of the United States Steel Corporation, and during some years, as much as one million dollars more for the goodwill and harmony which Mr. Schwab created among the workers because of his pleasing personality. His personality therefore was worth more than ten times as much as his brain and his experience—isn't that an astounding fact to know? Mr. Carnegie said that Mr. Schwab could go out into the shop or the factory, just walk through, not say anything, not look at anybody, not do anything, and everybody in the place would perform at least ten percent more work and better work the whole day, just as the result of his walking through there.

I will now begin to detail and illustrate the factors that make up a pleasing personality. The first factor which enters into a pleasing personality, ladies and gentlemen, is that of a positive mental attitude. That's number one, on the head of the list, and there's nothing any more important than that. A positive mental attitude, reflected in one's expression by words or thoughts or deeds, is determined by the emotions, among which the fourteen most important are as follows: The positive ones are faith, hope, love, enthusiasm, sex emotion, loyalty, and cheerfulness. The negative emotions are fear—that is to say, the seven basic fears: a fear of poverty, fear of ill health, fear of criticism, fear of the loss of love of someone, fear of the loss of personal liberty, fear of old age, and the fear of death. Your mental attitude is determined by which of these fourteen emotions dominate your mind.

Mental attitude attracts to you the physical counterparts of your dominating thoughts as surely as an electromagnet attracts steel filings. Keep your mental attitude positive at all times and you may make life pay off on your own terms.

A positive mental attitude: What does a person look like and act like who always maintains a positive mental attitude? Among other things, he always looks on the optimistic side of life. He accepts unpleasant circumstances in such a way that they do not discourage him. He looks for the best, expects the best, and if he receives the worst, he makes the most of it, but does not allow it to sour him.

He never gripes, he never complains, he never finds fault, although there may be much reason for his doing so.

The second factor that enters into a pleasing personality is that of flexibility. Flexibility is an astounding attribute. It is the ability to unbend, mentally and physically, and to adapt oneself to any circumstances or environment without loss of self-control or composure. I'll admit that that's a little difficult, but if you're going to have an attractive, pleasing personality, you'll have to be something like a rubber band. You'll have to be able to snap back every time somebody pulls you the wrong way.

If you'll study the great men that we've had in this country, those whom you've had a chance to study from their records, you'll find out that the ones that got along best were the ones that had the most flexible personalities. In the White House, for instance, I have known every president from Theodore Roosevelt on down to the present incumbent. I have had a chance to work with two of them closely; I've been in their administrations. I have had an opportunity to see what an important factor was this business of flexibility in the management of the greatest office in the world.

I will say that if Herbert Hoover had flexibility, if he'd been able to adjust himself to circumstances, had been able to unbend, he would have gone down in history as having been one of our very great presidents. As a matter of fact, he was a very great president, but he lost favor with the people because he couldn't unbend, and he couldn't adapt himself. He was inflexible in dealing with the causes and effects of the Great Depression.

Flexibility is a trait of the extrovert—that is to say, the person who can and does take a keen interest in people and expresses himself or herself freely. You never heard of an introvert being flexible. An introvert fixes his mind on his own selfish interests, and takes very little interest in other people. The flexible person also has full control of the emotions at all times. That's quite a statement, too: full control of the emotions at all times.

Factor number three is that of a pleasing tone of voice—that is to say, a voice controlled and cultivated to express any desired feeling, and free from sharp, nasal tones that indicate a fault-finding attitude. There are a lot of ways to say almost anything that you wish to say. I think you'll agree when I give you this little demonstration that it's not so much what you say that counts as it is the way you say it.

The most important speech in the world, the one most often spoken, consists of four words, and I'm going to make that speech for you in three different ways, to show you the importance of tone of voice, having a pleasing tone of voice. That speech is, "I love you, darling." If you say it very fast like this: "I love you, darling," that means to the wife or the sweetheart, "well, hurry and get ready; I'm impatient. I want to go." But if you say it too loud and dramatically, "I love you, darling," they'll know you're clowning. It won't mean a thing, and you'll be discounted. But if you say it slowly and softly, "I love you, darling," don't you think it would be interpreted very differently? Don't you think the tone of voice would convey to the person to whom you're speaking something that the words themselves do not convey?

When you're dealing with another person professionally, or in a business, like a doctor, for example, his medicines and his medical technique and his therapeutic technique, whatever it may be, all are important, but ladies and gentlemen, not half as important as what the doctor says in front of his patient. There are ways and means of a doctor conveying to his patient the feeling that the doctor thinks the patient is getting along all right, and is going to come through. There's another way of saying the same words so as to throw an awful scare into the patient, make him think he's going to die.

Tone of voice. Study your tone of voice. Record it on a recording machine and play it back over and over again. Take some sentence, like the one I just used: "I love you, darling." It won't hurt you to say that to your wife a lot of times. Find out the way she likes it best and you'll be surprised at what you can do by controlling your tone of voice.

Personally, I think one of the greatest weaknesses of the public school system is that hardly anybody ever comes out of public school knowing how to read aloud properly. I think it ought to be a must in all schools that all children should learn to become radio announcers. There are people who understand how to use their tone of voice properly, and how to read aloud properly. That's one of the outstanding factors of a pleasing personality: how to say things, how to dramatize words, how to make your tone of voice convey any kind of feeling that you choose.

The fourth factor in a pleasing personality is that of tolerance. Just plain tolerance: an open mind on all subjects toward all people at all times. That's quite an order, ladies and gentlemen: an open mind toward all people on all subjects at all times. Someone has said that when you close your mind, it's like a fruit on the tree that has become ripe. When fruit becomes ripe, the next stage is for it to fall off the tree and become rotten. As long as you remain green, however, you continue to grow. I like to feel that I shall always remain green, keep an open mind and keep on growing, because I doubt that a person lives who can truly say that he has or knows the last word on any subject. There's always something you may learn by keeping an open mind. If you look around you, however, you'll find a lot of closed minds that have been closed a long time, and perhaps they've rusted shut by this time and never could be opened again. I'm not speaking of my audience now; I don't think they're in that category. If they are, I wish to get them out of it.

The fifth factor in a pleasing personality is that of a keen sense of humor. Ladies and gentlemen, if you don't have a keen sense of humor, your life is going to be just like that of an elevator operator: a series of ups and downs. And you may be sure that you'll come down every time you go up. Learn to laugh. Learn to see the funny side of things. Learn to see the light side, and above all, don't take yourself or your business too seriously. Learn to relax, and be something of a humorist.

Number six, that factor is frankness of manner and speech, but frankness with discriminate control of the tongue at all times, based upon the habit of thinking before speaking. Many people speak first and think afterward—that is, sometimes they think afterward, but mostly they just speak, and let it go at that. Control of the tongue and measuring your words are so important. Wouldn't it be a wonderful thing if all people measured their words and held themselves to saying only the things that are beneficial, and nothing that is detrimental, nothing that is harmful or hurtful of other people?

I think one of the evils of our times, ladies and gentlemen, especially in the field of politics, is that the politicians generally do not seek office based upon the promotion of their own merits and virtues, but by tearing down their opponents, trying to blacken them. Frankness in manner and speech, with discriminate control over the tongue at all times . . . what a marvelous thing that is. I cannot over-emphasize the importance of controlling your tongue and keeping your tongue in your mouth unless you have something to say that might be helpful.

The seventh factor in a pleasing personality is that of a pleasing facial expression. Don't look like you're going to jump down a man's throat when you start talking to him. You can always soften up the message a little bit by smiling, whether you really feel that way or not. Here is a queer thing about this business of smiling: If you smile, even when you don't feel like it, why, pretty soon you'll commence feeling like it. It changes the chemistry of your body. Just smile. I think it's one of the grandest things in the world. I used to practice laughing out loud, in the bathroom. I didn't laugh very loud, you understand; I didn't want anybody to hear me. But I was in a job then where I took myself and my work too seriously. I wanted to learn to lighten up things a bit.

The eighth factor that enters into a pleasing personality is that of a keen sense of justice toward all people, applied in all human relationships, even when to do so may appear unprofitable. A keen sense of justice. You know, there are two or three or four different kinds of honesty, had you ever stopped to think about that? There is that type of honesty which you practice because you don't want to go to jail. There is another type of honesty which you practice because you do not wish to be in disrepute with your neighbors, people who know you. Then there is another kind of honesty that I think is the best one of all. That is that type through which you're honest because it does you good inside of your heart and soul to be that way regardless of the effects of it. I want to tell you, it does something to you. It strengthens your heart and your mind and your soul to know that you're inherently, intentionally honest about everything. When you go to grade yourself on that one, be very careful, you must be honest.

The ninth factor of a pleasing personality is that of sincerity of purpose in all human relationships. Remember that insincerity begets failure. Sincerity of purpose. I don't care whether a speaker uses the proper gestures or not. I don't care whether his posture is perfect or not. I don't care whether his English is perfect or not. If he puts across a message with a genuine feeling of sincerity, and you recognize that, you're going to overlook any of his imperfections. As for public speakers or conversationalists, there isn't anything in their personality that will do so much good as to reflect in their tone of voice, mental attitude, and words a spirit of sincerity of purpose.

The tenth factor of a pleasing personality is that of

versatility—that is to say, a wide range of knowledge of people and world events outside of your own immediate interests. I think one of the saddest things in the world is to come across a person who knows only one thing, and is not interested in finding out about anything else. In certain types of professions, for instance in bookkeeping in office work, men oftentimes become very expert at figures. But they are very indifferent to other things, and generally speaking, their personalities are not very attractive. That sometimes applies to the men engaged in the profession of the law. They know a great deal about the law. But they don't busy themselves with other things outside of their profession. They're not versatile.

I try to keep in touch with a little of everything that's going on throughout the whole world. Through the radio, through television, through magazines, through other reading, I try to keep myself informed on the important factors that are taking place all over the world. I devote a certain amount of time each day to that subject because I feel that I have to remain versatile. When I was doing the research, and building the science of success philosophy, I delved into every one of the sciences. I didn't master any of them, but I got a smattering of all of them. So when people start talking about the sciences, I at least know enough about them to understand what they are talking about.

The eleventh factor of a pleasing personality is that of tactfulness in speech and manner. Remember that not all thoughts should be expressed, even though they may be true. One of my wife's friends was describing a dress that a friend of hers had just bought, and telling my wife what a terrible color it was. She said, "Why, it was the most terrible, stupid, gaudy thing that I ever saw in my life." Then she reached over and took hold of the sleeve of a woman standing by who had a dress on similar to that and said, "Why, it was even worse than this one, right here." You can understand how much tact she had. Tactfulness in speech is important. There are so many things that you can say to hurt people, but you don't have to say them. Nothing against your thinking them if you want to, but you don't have to say things that hurt other people's feelings.

The twelfth factor is that of promptness of decision making. A dilly-dallier never gets anywhere, and he's never pleasing to anybody. I don't think so much of people who are not punctual with their appointments, either; I like to see people on time. If you want to be unpopular, just make it a habit to be always late, and I'm sure that very soon you're going to be discredited in a lot of other ways. Promptness of decision, promptness in keeping appointments, promptness in doing anything that you're going to do, not dilly-dallying around, is important.

The thirteenth factor of a pleasing personality is that

of faith in infinite intelligence, based upon observation of the orderliness of the visible portion of the world and the universe around you, and natural laws. I personally don't think that anybody would be entirely popular, have an entirely pleasing personality in this age of enlightenment, who didn't recognize the existence of a first cause, or of infinite intelligence. That's an essential part of a pleasing personality. You don't have to go around talking about it, or have a sign pinned on your shoulder declaring to the world that you believe in infinite intelligence, but you have to live and adjust yourself to the natural laws of life in such a way as to demonstrate that you believe in it. Incidentally, it'll be not only helpful in causing other people to like you, but it'll be helpful to you in getting through life with the least amount of resistance.

The fourteenth factor that enters into a pleasing personality is that of the appropriateness of words used, free from slang, wisecracks, and profanity. There has sprung up in the generation coming along right now a tendency toward wisecracking, punning, trying to be funny, clowning. That may be funny at times, but if you make a habit of it people are going to resent it. The English language is a beautiful language. It's very expressive; it's not so easy to master. But if you use it properly, you'll always be more effective in speech than if you try to pun, wisecrack, or use profanity.

The fifteenth factor of a pleasing personality is that of controlled enthusiasm, the ability to turn on and off your enthusiasm at will, with a special attention to enthusiasm in speech. Enthusiasm may be either passive or active. Passive enthusiasm is the kind that you feel inside of you, that gives you action and initiative, and puts your imagination to work, but doesn't get you into difficulty with other people because you've said too much or said it at the wrong time. Enthusiasm is one of the seventeen principles of success, and in my books we regard it as controlled enthusiasm. It is something that you turn on when you want to arouse the interest of the other fellow who's listening, and something that you turn off before you start boring him.

Well, ladies and gentlemen, I have plenty more enthusiasm left tonight, but have run out of time. Join me next week for a further discussion of the importance of a pleasing personality.

11

MORE FACTORS OF A PLEASING PERSONALITY

How do you do, everyone. Thanks for joining me again. Last time we met I discussed fifteen of the twenty-five major factors of a pleasing personality. Tonight I will discuss the remaining ten, and will tell you fifteen things you cannot do if you hope to have a pleasing personality.

Number sixteen is good, clean sportsmanship. Nobody likes a poor loser. If presidential candidate Al Smith had been a good loser, and hadn't gone around like a big, angered guy when he was defeated in 1928, he probably would have gotten another chance at it, and might have become president of the United States. Be a good loser. Nobody likes a bad loser. You never in the world saw a man profit by showing indignation or resentment over having been a loser. Aren't we all losers at one time or another in life? Doesn't it pay all of us to learn to be good losers? The good loser has a chance to come back again; the bad loser seldom has that chance.

Number seventeen in the factors making up a pleasing personality is common courtesy, just common, plain, everyday, garden variety, old-fashioned courtesy, both in speech and in one's mental attitude. Perhaps never an hour goes by in a whole day that you don't have a chance to be courteous or discourteous. Don't let a chance go by. Always express courtesy.

We have now factor number eighteen which enters into the maintenance of a pleasing personality, and this is appropriateness of personal adornment. Adornment should suit the nature of one's work and social activities. And I might say to the gentlemen of the audience that zoot suits are out. I might say to the ladies of the audience that certain types of hats are out. Appropriateness of adornment— that's a wonderful thing, to adorn yourself appropriately to your calling, or to the work in which you are engaged for the moment.

There are times when, if you came to call on me, you'd find me in overalls, maybe a sports shirt; maybe I might not even have on any kind of a shirt. I'd be out in my garden, getting a sunbath and some good physical exercise and enjoying myself, all at the same time. But if I came onto the stage lecturing in that kind of garb, I suspect that I would go down as an eccentric person, if not worse. So there is no one rule as to what appropriateness consists of. That depends upon each occasion and the work or circumstance in which you're engaged.

The nineteenth factor of a pleasing personality is that of good showmanship, based on the ability to say and do the right thing at the right time to attract favorable attention to oneself. There are a lot of ways of attracting attention to yourself. For instance, I could go down here on Main Street and stand on my head in the middle of the street and hold up traffic, maybe get myself a traffic violation ticket, and attract quite a lot of notoriety. But it wouldn't be favorable, would it?

I can think of a lot of ways that I could attract attention. I could do it with eccentricities of adornment, as I have seen some speakers do. I could do it by letting my hair grow long, down around my shoulders, pretending that it was being pushed out by brains. But I doubt that would be of any value to me. It wouldn't, it would be showmanship, but not good showmanship. Good showmanship consists of a technique that you work out for yourself, to keep yourself before the particular audience that you wish to be sold to, whatever that happens to be. It could be your neighbors or your business associates, your clients or your patients, or whomsoever it may be.

The twentieth factor that enters into a pleasing personality is the habit of going the extra mile. I don't mean just doing that once or twice, but I mean adopting this outstanding principle as one of your habits, and making it your business never to let a day go by that you don't apply this habit in one way or another. It could be nothing more than calling somebody on the telephone that you know and haven't seen or talked to for some time, and expressing your good wishes for him, and the hope that he's happy and well. That wouldn't hurt you, wouldn't cost you very much, to make one or two such telephone calls every day.

If I were a doctor, I'm pretty sure that every so often I'd call up all of my past patients and wish them well. It might cut into the pocketbook a little for the time being, but eventually it would pay off. Let the patient know that your interest in him has not ceased just because he got well. You might even congratulate him for having selected the right doctor, so he could get well so quickly.

Factor number twenty-one in a pleasing personality is that of temperance, temperance in eating and drinking, and in work and play, and in thinking. Temperance. It's not going to hurt you to take a cocktail, if you want one, if you don't take too many, and if you don't take them at the wrong time. It's not going to hurt you to smoke a few cigars, if you don't smoke too many. It's not going to hurt you to eat a nice meal if you don't eat too much. You can do just as much damage overeating food as you can over-drinking alcoholic beverages or oversmoking. Temperance in all things, a balanced life, is essential to a pleasing personality. One of the reasons, ladies and gentlemen, that I have such an overabundance of enthusiasm and endurance and physical health at all times at my age is that I have myself balanced through temperance of living. Not too much, not too little of anything, but enough of everything. What would be enough for me wouldn't be enough for you, perhaps. Each individual must study his own life, and find out what temperance for him would really be.

Factor number twenty-two is that of patience under all circumstances, patience and understanding of people. Patience is a willingness to recognize that because the other fellow's not living the way you would have him live, that there may be a very good reason for it. Patience with the fellow who doesn't seem to know as much about life as you know. Patience with the motorist on the highway who doesn't seem to drive as well as you can drive—and I have never seen a man yet who thought that any other motorist could drive as well as he could. Patience and understanding are two of the outstanding virtues of people who have a pleasing personality. Not condemning other people because you do not agree with them. In the rearing of children, and in dealing with elderly people, you've got to be patient. You've got to be understanding. It doesn't take very much willpower to be patient under all circumstances, with all people.

Young people starting out, or anybody starting out in a new job, must have a lot of patience, because you don't start at the top. If you did, it would be very bad for you, because there would be only one way that you could move. You start at the bottom, and if you are patient and go the extra mile and do the right thing, eventually you'll be up at the top.

The twenty-third factor entering into a pleasing personality is that of gracefulness in posture and carriage of the body. I hate to see people lounging around, looking sloppy and acting sloppy in their posture. It's a nice thing to be graceful in your movements in walking and in your posture in sitting or standing. It doesn't need to be the studied posture of an actor, but nevertheless, it can at least be graceful.

The twenty-fourth factor of a pleasing personality is that of humility of the heart, based upon a keen sense of modesty. Humility of the heart, isn't that a wonderful thing? I think perhaps, ladies and gentlemen, the reason that I didn't get recognition, that fame didn't come to me in the early days of my life, is that I wouldn't have been able to stand it then like I do now. I had to acquire humility of the heart. To have been recognized by 65 million people throughout two thirds of the civilized world thirty years ago perhaps would have turned my personality into one that wouldn't be very pleasing. I've been thankful that such recognition and fame as have come to me came at a time only after I had gained humility of the heart. I couldn't be spoiled nowadays with money, nor with acclaim, nor with applause, nor with anything else that I can think of, because I do have humility of the heart.

The twenty-fifth factor is that of personal magnetism, an inborn trait and the only one of the traits of personality which cannot be cultivated. But it can be controlled and directed to beneficial usages. When I speak of personal magnetism, let's understand each other: I'm speaking primarily of the emotion of sex, that great, creative, constructive emotion which is responsible for the growth and advancement of the world.

Speaking of personalities, of people, I wonder if you would ever stop to think that homes and stores and offices and places of businesses and streets and towns and cities all have personalities, separate and distinct from one another. You go down Fifth Avenue in New York City, and you'll get one feeling from the personality of Fifth Avenue, which is a feeling of opulence. Even though you may not have much money in your pocket, you'll not feel poor. You'll mix and mingle with the people who are patronizing those great shops there on Fifth Avenue, and you'll feel for the time being that, while you may not be rich, you are at least not poor. You walk five blocks over toward the Hudson River, into what is known as Hell's Kitchen, where people live and think and exist in misery and in poverty, and I don't care who you are, the chances are that if you stay over there ten minutes you'll feel like you want to scream, because of the negative vibrations that are being released over there.

You must remember that your brain is both a broadcasting station and a receiving station, and your mental attitude, whatever it may be, is constantly being broadcast to other people. If you don't learn to keep your mental attitude positive, other people will pick it up and hand it right back to you as their mental attitude in a negative form. Isn't that an amazing and important thing to recognize?

Once I had a man come to enroll in my school of salesmanship in Chicago. He said, "Mr. Hill, I came a thousand miles to let you sell me. You start right in and give me a good selling, because I want to go into the sales business." And then he kept talking. He had asked me to talk, but then he did the talking. He talked for almost an hour. Meantime, I was talking back to him, but I was talking mentally, not orally. When he got through talking, he got up and we shook hands, and he said, "This course is the very thing that I want, and I thank you for your marvelous sales talk, and you get out your enrollment blank, and

I'll enroll." I hadn't opened my mouth. But I had been conveying thoughts to him, very definitely. Learn the art of projecting your thoughts to wherever you wish them to go, and see to it that those thoughts are always constructive and beneficial to other people. When you come into contact with those other people, you'll find that their thoughts and acts directed back toward you will be friendly.

There has never been a master salesman who didn't send his mind ahead of him when he went out to make a sale. He went there ahead of him and conditioned the mind of his prospective buyer long before he came into contact with that prospective buyer. All master salesmen do that. Those who do not do it are not master salesmen. They're order takers, perhaps, but not master salesmen.

Here are some examples of a pleasing personality: I've already spoken to you about Charles M. Schwab. Mr. Schwab had very little schooling, but he had a very magnetic personality, and he had the ability to turn on his personal charm when he was talking to other people. As a result of that, Mr. Carnegie oftentimes paid him more than ten times as much for that personality as he paid him for the mere use of his skill and his brains.

Franklin D. Roosevelt had a marvelous personality, a million-dollar personality on the radio alone. It was so great that it gave him four terms in the White House, a circumstance without precedent in our nation. I would say that ninety percent of the reason why he was elected for the fourth term was due to that appealing personality that he had. If you'll go back and grade him as you remember him by each of these twenty-five factors, you'll find that he scores practically one hundred percent on every one of them, including the control of his tone of voice.

Kate Smith's mental attitude brings her more income than the president of the United States receives. Kate's not a singer in the true sense of the word, as are some of the great opera stars. She's a songster, and a star of radio and television. I'd say she's a sweet songster—I started to say a sweet, little songster, but I couldn't quite describe her in just that way. She is a large woman. She has a sweet personality, she has a sweet tone of voice in which she speaks, and no matter whether you like the song she's singing or not, you like the one who is doing the singing, and that's the important thing in life.

Whenever you open your mouth to say something, if the person to whom you're saying it doesn't like what you're saying, at least try to say it in such a way that he will like the person who's saying it. A man by the name of Pappy O'Daniel, a flower salesman, took his family and some musical instruments and barnstormed the state of Texas, sang on the radio and made himself governor of that great state, and later United States senator. The biggest thing that he had to commend him to the people for election to those two high offices that he held was his charming personality, and his ability to turn on that charm, and to keep it on whenever he was speaking, regardless of whether his audience liked what he said.

Will Rogers joked his way into a fortune, not to mention the hearts of the American people, because of that marvelous personality of his.

Now let us consider some of the things that you shall not do if you want to have a pleasing personality. We'll get both sides of the picture. In other words, these are the don'ts, and there are fifteen of them. First is the habit of breaking in when others are speaking. That's absolutely on the don't list. If you want to have a pleasing personality, if you want people to like you, when they're speaking wait until they slow down before jumping in and taking away the conversation. I suspect there's not a person in my audience, either the radio audience or in this studio, who couldn't point to half a dozen people who make themselves very obnoxious by dominating all conversations and never allowing the other fellow to do any talking. If you want to be popular, learn the art of being a good listener, and incidentally, always when you're listening, you're learning something. When you're talking, you're never learning anything, because you're only saying and hearing that which you already know.

Number two, selfishness expressed by words or deeds

is on the don't list. You may have a selfish feeling inside of you. If you do, try to conquer it as fast as you can. Certainly, don't give any outward expression to it.

Third on the don't list, no sarcasm should be used, either expressed by words or by deeds. There is also a way of expressing sarcasm not by words or by deeds, but by the expression on your face. It may give you a good deal of personal satisfaction to blow off steam and express sarcasm in connection with things you don't like, but it's not going to make you popular.

Number four, exaggeration of speech, that's on the don't list. It's far better to understate a truth than it is to overstate it. Be on the conservative side. If you go one iota beyond what people believe to be a reasonable statement, they'll discount your whole statement.

Number five is egotism expressed in actual or implied self-praise. That's out, that's on the don't list. Any kind of self-praise, whether it's by direct words or by actions, is taboo.

Number six on the don't list is indifference toward others and their interests. If you really and truly want to be popular, you must find out what other people are interested in and start them to talking to you about those things while you become a good listener. And brother, sister, you can violate about every one of these other rules and get by nicely if you can become a good listener and interest yourself in what other people have to say.

I'll never forget, as long as I live, the first visit I made to the White House, when Theodore Roosevelt was president. I was just a youngster, but he took me into his office, gave me a nice big chair, a padded chair by the side of the presidential seat, turned around and faced me, slapped me on the shoulder, and he sat there and talked to me just like I was as important as the president of the United States. For the time being, I forgot that I wasn't. I never did forget that. I learned, subsequently, by studying the really great men that I had the privilege of working with, that they all had that great capacity of making you feel at home. They were never indifferent. They were good listeners.

The next factor, number seven, envy expressed or implied by action, is out. It's a don't. If you're going to be envious of other people, if you're going to be envious of the people in your town or your neighborhood who've attained a degree of success perhaps somewhat beyond yours, you're not going to be liked by those people, you're not going to be liked by your neighbors, you're not going to be liked by anybody, because nobody likes an envious person. Envy should be converted into gratitude. Whenever you see another person that has something that you would like to have but don't, express gratitude in your heart that the other fellow does have it, and hope that you can catch up with him and be able to get that for yourself later on. But envy, no.

The eighth factor is that of expressing flattery where it is not justified. If you want to be misunderstood, if you want to be discounted, start flattering somebody beyond the point at which he knows he's entitled to your flattery, and you'll certainly excite his suspicion very quickly. In my public career, I have come into contact with all kinds of people. Most of my students have been most generous in expressing their recognition of what I have given to the world. Most of them have been very considerate, and very, very few of them have gone beyond the point of stopping their expression of flattery or recognition at about the point where I'm entitled to it. Any time that you start to over-flatter a person, you excite his suspicions, and he tightens up on you. He thinks you're after something, and generally speaking, that suspicion is not without a foundation.

One of my contemporary motivational authors wrote a book, and the major point in the book is that you get ahead in life by flattering people. I'd say that was one of the oldest tricks in the world, and one of the most dangerous. Giving credit to people where it does not belong, or over expressing it to them, is on the don't list.

Number nine is slovenliness in speech. You don't have to be perfect in your grammar, but you at least ought to know how to use language with reasonable accuracy. That is especially true if you're going to engage in any kind of public life, where you regularly come into contact with people.

Number ten is the habit of monopolizing conversations, not letting the other fellow get a word in crosswise. You may be a great conversationalist; you may have a lot of things to say that are interesting. But if you don't know when to stop, and if you don't give the other fellow a chance to come up once in a while with a few expressions of his own, you'll never learn anything about the other fellow; you'll never learn what his reactions to you are. A good salesman never fails to take note of the effect that his words are having upon the person doing the listening. A poor salesman memorizes his talk and he reels it off like a canned program, never stopping to see what affect it's having on the audience.

If you want to have a pleasing personality, be sure that the person to whom you are speaking is listening, and listening with interest. You want to be a lecturer, for instance? You never in the world could be a successful lecturer unless you kept your finger on the pulse of your entire audience. You would know at every instance when your talk was going over, and you would know the very second that it was not, and you would change your trend of that talk if it were not going over and registering properly.

I have had lectures when I had to change the trend of my talk three or four times. I was lecturing to a group of nurses down in Atlanta, Georgia, once on the law of cosmic habit force. I'd been going about ten minutes when I saw that I wasn't even hitting near the mark, let alone hitting the bull's-eye, with my talk. I just stopped dead right there and I said, "Ladies, I wish to ask you a question. I want to know what's wrong with you or me. I know it's with one or the other of us, because you're not a darn bit interested in what I'm saying." That broke the ice, and then we changed the trend of the talk over to how to succeed in a difficult profession, and brother, sister, did I get attention then. I really got it.

Number eleven, this is on the don't list, is trying to convey an impression of superiority. You may be superior to other people, and the chances are that all of you are superior to somebody that you know. But it's not good breeding, it's not good manners, it's not good business, it's not good fellowship to try to convey to anybody the fact that you're superior to him. No matter how humble the man may be, he doesn't want that rubbed into him by somebody whom he knows to be superior.

Number twelve, insincerity in general, is on the don't list. Number thirteen, the habit of directing conversation to cheap gossip, is on the list. I don't know whether you ever heard of anybody who did that, or who does that, or not. But I am sure that if you did, none of them are among your friends today. They are the ones who are talking about us, directing conversation to cheap gossip. You can waste most of your life talking about things that are not of any benefit to you nor to anyone else.

I think perhaps one of the greatest compliments ever paid me by one of my fellow men was paid by Dr. William P. Jacobs, president of Presbyterian College in South Carolina, with whom I was associated for a time while I was on the staff of that college. After he had known me about six months, he said, "Dr. Hill, do you know what I like best about you?" I said, "No, Dr. Jacobs, I don't, but I'd like to know." He said, "You don't engage in small talk." Well, I said, "I thank you. I thought maybe sometimes I did." He said, "If you do, I have never heard you."

I don't mean that you should always engage in abstractions or in deep conversations, but you should stay off of the gossipy side.

Fourteen, the habit of fault finding with the individual and the world at large is a don't. You can go down into Skid Row in any city, and you can find out what's the matter with the president, what's wrong with his administration, what's wrong with the United States government, and what's wrong with God. Anything you want to know, they have it down there in Skid Row. But who wants to be in Skid Row? I don't even want to pass through there, let alone engage in conversation with them. They are people who have soured on life. They find fault with everything and everybody, and believe nobody likes them. That's perhaps why they're in Skid Row. They didn't look for the positive side of life.

And next and last, number fifteen, is the habit of challenging people with whom you do not agree. You don't have to challenge people because you don't agree with them. Quietly listen to the things that they think and believe and say, unless it's directly your responsibility to challenge them. Then, when you do it, do it softly.

I thank you for your attention tonight and last time, and hope I have given you some insights into how to have a pleasing personality. I gave you a lot of do's and don'ts to consider. Please reflect on them, and grade yourself honestly against them. You may be surprised at how you stack up.

Please join me next time for the first of two broadcasts focusing on the supreme law of the universe, cosmic habit force.

12

COSMIC HABIT FORCE

The subject of this broadcast and the next one, our final programs in Paris, is cosmic habit force. I don't want you to become scared on account of the high-sounding name, but before I finish, I hope to convey to you that this is one of the most important, if not the most important, principles of this entire success series.

Some years ago, shortly after *Think and Grow Rich* was published, I began to get letters and telegrams from all over the world complimenting me on that book. Those letters and telegrams became so numerous that I sent my secretary out to get a copy of it. I hadn't read it since I wrote it some year and a half before that. I sat down and read it. I read it carefully. While I was reading, I discovered in that book, not on the lines but behind the lines, this marvelous subject on which we're speaking tonight, the law of cosmic habit force.

I want to tell you that the major purpose of all my books, including *Think and Grow Rich*, and of my personal lectures, is not necessarily to tell people that which they don't already know, but to inspire them to use their own minds, and to make a better use of the things they already know. I want you to know that's the purpose of this talk tonight.

Cosmic habit force is a law of the universe into which all of the other natural laws blend and become a part. It's the comptroller of all of the natural laws, you might say. I want to tell you that there are three factors that enter into it that are quite important. These three factors are, first of all, as I have called to your attention many times, nature has given to every individual the most precious thing available to mankind, and this thing which has been given to mankind by nature has never been given to any other living creature. It is nothing more nor less than the power of control over one's mind. Second, nature has provided mankind with the means by which he may organize this great privilege of using his own mind, and direct it to any end he pleases. The means by which this may be done is the law of cosmic habit force. The third factor is that in order to make use of this law, there must be a technique, a plan, a method.

I don't know that my plan is the best one in the world, but it has been successful in connection with my own life and my own work. I call it the eight guiding princes. The first of those eight guiding princes is the prince of financial prosperity. I have never yet found any way of getting along in life in any station or calling above mediocrity without finances, and I don't believe anybody else can do it. I'll correct myself on that. I knew one man who, despite the fact that he didn't have any money, didn't have any military forces, didn't even own a suit of clothes, nevertheless brought about the freedom of a great nation. That man was Mahatma Gandhi. He got along all right without money, but personally, I've never been able to do it. So the prince of financial prosperity heads the list of these guiding princes that I have created in my own mind for the purpose of taking advantage of this great law of cosmic habit force which, once it is established, automatically carries out whatever purpose you direct it to.

Number two of these princes is the prince of sound physical health. In the work in which I am engaged, I have to demonstrate sound physical health all the time. I put a tremendous amount of energy into everything I do, and especially into my writing. I write under inspiration; I have to key myself up, and I'll tell you that when I go to key myself down, I oftentimes am exhausted. So I have to have sound physical health.

The third of these princes is the prince of peace of mind. I learned a long time ago that there wasn't any real purpose in wasting your energy in worrying about things, in fretting about things, or in fearing things. So I created this prince of peace of mind for the purpose of clearing my mind and keeping it clear of those little things which annoy people so much. I think the thing that caused me to give so much attention to the importance of peace of mind was that I read a little statement once which said that a man is no bigger than the things which he allows to annoy him. I made up my mind I was going to set up in my mind the means of avoiding these little, petty circumstances which have the effect of annoying people.

The next two of these eight princes are twins; they are called the prince of hope and the prince of faith. Their purpose is to give me inspired guidance. They tell me what to do and what not to do. I don't always follow their guidance, I might tell you that. When I don't, I generally get into difficulty.

The next two are also twins; they are the princes of love and romance. Their duty is simply to keep me young in body and mind, and now when I have a birthday, I not only do not add another year, but I take off a year. And I might tell you, I'm getting to be in my second childhood, already.

The last and the most important of these eight guiding princes is the prince of overall wisdom. The purpose and object of the prince of overall wisdom is to keep the other seven princes working on my behalf, and also to connect me to all of the circumstances which affect my life in such a way that I benefit by those circumstances.

The reason I go over the identity and role of these eight princes is to let you know the particular technique by which I have chosen to make use of this great law of cosmic habit force. This law explains the importance of habits in our lives. It's interesting to know how habits are formed. I read a little piece not long ago which says: "Vice is a monster of so frightful a mien that to be hated, it needs but to be seen. Yet seen too oft, familiar with her face, we first endure, then pity, and then embrace." That's the way bad habits are formed, a little at a time.

I saw something in a journal not long ago that fitted into this lesson tonight beautifully. In one sentence, the writer says that habit is at first like a cobweb. Then it grows to be a strong cable with which many people bind themselves for life. What an interesting and correct statement that is.

The purpose of this broadcast and the next is to describe the law by which one acquires habits, a law so stupendous in its scope and power that it may be difficult of understanding, except by those who have a comprehensive knowledge of the sciences. This law is known as cosmic habit force—that is, the ultimate principle pertaining to the universe and the laws which govern it. This is the law by which the equilibrium of the whole universe is maintained in orderliness through established habits. This law forces every living thing and every inanimate particle of matter to adhere to and follow the pattern of its environment, including the physical habits and the thinking habits of mankind.

Here are some of the fixed habits of cosmic habit force: First of all, there are the stars and the planets as they are established in their fixed places in the heavens. Isn't it a marvelous thing to contemplate the orderliness of this whole universe, and to recognize that their habits are so definitely fixed—that is, the habits of the stars and the planets—that astronomers may estimate and determine hundreds of years in advance the exact relationship of any two given stars or planets? Nature doesn't do anything by rule of thumb. She has definite ways of doing everything. She has laws by which she governs the universe, and those laws apply to individuals as well.

We see the law of cosmic habit force working out in the seasons of the year. They come and go with regularity, and sometimes we can anticipate what they're going to be like in advance, but not always—at least, not here in this particular community. And we see it in the reproduction and growth of everything that sprouts from the soil of the earth, with each seed reproducing precisely its own kind, without variation, and in the reproduction of every living thing from the smallest insect and the microscopic particle on up to man. You never heard of a farmer planting a grain of wheat and raising a stalk of corn, or vice versa. You never heard of a pine seed producing an oak tree. Nature has definite ways of doing everything according to fixed habits that are inexorable and cannot be circumvented, cannot be avoided.

We see it in the chemical actions of matter, from the smallest particles of matter, which are the electrons and protons of the atom, to the largest particles of matter as they exist in the stars in the heavens. All actions and reactions of matter are based upon the fixed habits of cosmic habit force.

Everything that has life in this world, with the lone exception of man, comes into life with its life span and its actions and reactions fixed in a definite pattern, through what we call instinct. Man is the only one who comes to life with no fixed pattern, and with the ability to establish and carry out his own pattern, by adapting himself to this great law of cosmic habit force. Yet this law ultimately governs even the thought habits of individuals, which are automatically fixed and made permanent by cosmic habit force, no matter whether they are negative or positive. The individual creates the pattern of his thoughts by repetition of thought on any given subject. But the law of cosmic habit force takes over these patterns and makes them permanent unless they are broken up by the will of the individual. Man is the only living creature that is equipped with the power to rearrange these at will.

Therefore, let us consider briefly some of the practical applications one may make of this great benefit. Let us consider some of the focal points at which you should begin establishing habits of your own making, thus taking advantage of the great law of cosmic habit force in carrying out these habits.

I might say to you that you are who you are and what you are today as a result of the habits that you've been accumulating, back down through the past. Probably the vast majority of those habits were fixed upon you not necessarily by design, but by the circumstances of your environment, as the result of the influences that you have come into contact with. Unless you are outstanding and unusual, instead of taking advantage of this great prerogative which nature gave you, the right to control your mind, to make your mind whatever you wish it to be, you probably have never taken full possession of your entire mind. You have never probably recognized the fact that there are great rewards awaiting you if you do this, and great penalties also awaiting you if you do not.

Here is where cosmic habit force should be applied to

definite circumstances in order to take possession of your own mind, and to direct it to whatever destiny you want to carry out. I want you to observe very carefully how well this principle fits in with principles discussed on previous broadcasts, especially definiteness of purpose. Because the first place where you want to start using the law of cosmic habit force is in connection with definiteness of purpose. You want to begin by deciding on that definite major purpose, talking to yourself about it, and dealing with your subconscious mind exactly as if it were another person.

When I start talking to the eight princes in connection with any objective I wish to attain in life, I deal with them just as if they were real people. I don't always talk out loud where people can hear me, because I don't want them turning their fingers around at their temples and saying, "There's another good man gone wrong." Very often, I carry out my instructions to my eight princes in silence, generally just before I go to sleep. I talk to them just as if they were paid servants of mine, and I don't get rough with them, I don't think that would help any. The most that I do is call their attention to my needs, and express my gratitude in advance for having received and responded to my requests. That's highly important.

Definiteness of purpose is the beginning point where you'll learn to make the most profitable use of this great law of cosmic habit force. Draw a clear picture of the thing you wish to attain in life, the person you wish to be, the place you wish to go, and then repeat that in your mind many hundreds of times a day until cosmic habit force has a chance to pick up that picture and automatically work it into a habit. You'll find that after that is accomplished practically everything and every circumstance that confronts you will bring you nearer and nearer to the object of your purpose, whatever it may be.

This applies not only to your major or overall or outstanding purpose, but it applies as well to your minor purposes. The major portion of the people of the world don't have a definite purpose. They drift along, following the path of least resistance. They're going around and around just like a goldfish in a bowl, always coming back to the place from whence they started and coming back empty-handed. You don't need any elaborate proof of this, you only need to look around and examine the people you know best, and you'll find that that's true.

If you will examine any person who is outstanding in any field, any calling, any profession, any business, any industry, you'll discover that that person has a definite major objective, and that he devotes the major portion of his time to carrying out that objective. He eats it, he sleeps it, he thinks about it, he takes it to bed with him, he gets up with it of a morning. He takes it to his work with him. It becomes an intimate part of his companionship. Only by doing that can you be absolutely sure of the law of cosmic habit force taking over your objective and working out definite ways and means of helping you to attain it.

There is a law in the universe known as the law of harmonious attraction. That law states that like attracts like. If you're a negative-minded person, you're going to attract other negative-minded persons, and my, my what a gossip fest they oftentimes have when they get together. If you're a positive-minded person, you will have fewer neighbors and friends, perhaps, but they'll be only positive-minded people. You won't attract the negatives. The agency through which this law operates is none other than the great overall law of cosmic habit force.

The next place to apply cosmic habit force is establishing the definite routine for developing a health consciousness. You don't just develop a health consciousness by wanting to be healthy—everybody wishes to be healthy. No, I beg your pardon, that isn't true. There are people who enjoy poor health, and we call them a $64 word: hypochondriacs. But generally speaking, other than the hypochondriac, most people want sound physical health, but I fear they don't have the best of knowledge as to how to go about getting that.

If you want to have sound physical health, you've got to think in terms of health. Stop imagining that you're suffering with all kinds of ailments, like the hypochondriac does. You've got to work at that. You've got to think about it day in and day out. I never go to bed at night that I don't sit down on the side of my bed and express my gratitude to the prince of sound physical health for keeping me in such fine condition. If perchance I do get up with a bad headache of a morning, which is very rare, I immediately go back to trace the cause, and I get right after the prince of sound physical health and ask him to do something about that cause. So far, he hasn't let me down.

The next practical application of cosmic habit force is the development and the maintenance of a positive mental attitude. Ladies and gentlemen, you don't get a positive mental attitude by allowing all of the circumstances of life to fix themselves upon you whether you want them to or not. I've heard people say, "Well, I had an experience today with a certain person, which made me very angry." Ladies and gentlemen, nobody is going to make me angry unless I wish to become angry, because I have a system of keeping my mind positive, of keeping things that would ordinarily annoy people or anger people out of my mind. I don't react to them. I do react, but just as if they didn't happen. I do not permit them to destroy my system of maintaining a positive mental attitude.

As the result of this particular principle, you may be interested in knowing that within the last fourteen years, since I discovered the law of cosmic habit force and began to use it, I have placed myself in a position in life where I have everything in the world that I want or need or can possibly use, including peace of mind, including sound physical health, including the joy of being of service to people, in writing books and delivering lectures. Prior to that time, I had just as much knowledge about the science of success as I now have, but I didn't have peace of mind, I didn't have sound physical health; I didn't have a lot of things because I hadn't worked out a definite way of establishing a positive mental attitude, and keeping it positive at all times.

The next application of cosmic habit force is the habit of taking personal inventory periodically, perhaps every six months, to develop an accurate listing of all your assets and liabilities, including both tangible and intangible things. If you're going to understand yourself, if you're going to be prosperous and if you're going to have peace of mind, you've got to know what are your assets and liabilities— and I am not talking about banking assets and liabilities alone. I'm talking about things that are even more important than anything that could be banked. I'm talking about your recognition, if you please, of that great gift from the Creator which permits you to use your mind any way you choose to use it. I'm also talking about your privilege of directing your mind to whatever you wish to attain, with the assurance that you're going to be able to attain it. I have never yet met a successful person in any calling that hadn't discovered that he owned his own mind, and hadn't discovered that he had the power to direct that mind to the attainment of any goal he might seek.

I was greatly surprised when I first met Henry Ford. I observed that he had a very weak personality, I learned that he had little formal schooling, I noticed he had some peculiar opinions, and I wondered how in the name of heaven, a man like that would have attained so much success. That is, I wondered until I became acquainted with Mr. Ford, and I found out that he had stumbled upon a way of recognizing the power of his own mind, and built for himself a plan of making use of that discovery by directing it to whatever he wished to attain. I asked Mr. Ford once if he had ever really and truly desired anything which he hadn't been able to acquire. With a sly grin on his face, he said, "Yes, one time. When I was in high school I wanted a certain redheaded girl for a wife, and the other fellow got her." I said, "Was that all?" He said, "Well, yes, that was all. Everything else I have wanted, I have been able to get." I said, "Have you always been able to get the things you wanted without struggle?" He said, "No, I don't think anybody ever reaches that point." But he said, "Struggle to me is just a way of becoming stronger. And I find that every time I refuse to yield to struggle, I become stronger the next time in connection with the same circumstance."

I heard a similar story from Mr. Edison, and from

Mr. Wanamaker, the department store tycoon. I heard similar stories of struggle and success from at least four hundred of those five hundred outstanding Americans who helped build the Science of Success. These men recognized this great prerogative given to them by the Creator, their right to take possession of their mind, to use it, to set up in that mind thought patterns of their own choosing, and to stand by until cosmic habit force guided them through the ways and means of carrying out those thought patterns.

The next practical application of cosmic habit force is the development of a system for applying the principle of going the extra mile, in your job or in your profession, or in your relationships generally with people. It's just not enough, ladies and gentlemen, for you to understand the principle of going the extra mile and say, "Yes, I believe in that." That's not enough. You know, practically everybody believes in the Golden Rule, but the way some interpret it, it means doing it to the other fellow and doing it to him plenty hard before he does it to you. Yes, they believe in going the extra mile, but the person who is a student of the Science of Success philosophy recognizes that you have to have a system, a technique, a method of honestly and fairly applying this principle of going the extra mile. One of the things you do is to start moving on that principle right where you stand, with whatever circumstance that may be nearest to you. Start on it without thought of what you're going to get back in return.

I want to tell you that of all the success laws that I know anything about, I don't know of one that brings back such great returns in such a variety of assets as this principle of going the extra mile. But you've got to start practicing it, and keep on practicing, without stopping to wonder how much you're going to get out of it. If you apply the principle of going the extra mile today, and then expect that you're going to get a reward tomorrow, it would be just like a farmer who went out and planted his wheat today, and the next day he went out with his harvesting machinery, ready to harvest the crop, and was surprised to not find any wheat. The farmer recognizes that there's an element of timing which enters between the planting and the harvesting, and that's true with reference to the service you render in going the extra mile.

When you once get into the habit of doing that, rendering extra services without expecting immediate results, that great law of harmonious attractions, that great law of increasing returns, begins to work in your behalf. Whether you will it or not, the things that are good for you, the things that you desire most, begin to come to you, and they come oftentimes from the most unexpected sources, because that law of cosmic habit force has taken over the pattern which you set up by your daily actions in going the extra mile, and has begun to carry it out. That's the way the law works.

Ladies and gentlemen, our time is up for tonight. Please join me next week for further discussion of the law of cosmic habit force.

13

FURTHER APPLICATION OF THE LAW OF COSMIC HABIT FORCE

Thank you for joining me for my final broadcast in this series here in Paris. Tonight I will complete the discussion of this supreme principle, the law of cosmic habit force.

I have been illustrating how to practically apply this law. The next application is using cosmic habit force to develop a system for budgeting and making better use of your time. Procrastination can be conquered, and procrastination, as you may know, is one of the major enemies of all mankind.

Many of you ladies and gentlemen have heard me speak of the affliction of my second son, my son Blair, who was born without any signs of ears. When Blair was born, the doctors who delivered him told me that he would be a deaf and dumb mute all his life. I never accepted that edict; I didn't accept it at the beginning, I haven't ever accepted it since. As a result of my application of the law of cosmic habit force, although I didn't know the law existed at that time, I devoted some nine years to working on my son, with the result that I induced nature to improvise a hearing system for him which gave him sixty-five percent of his natural hearing. I want to tell you that called forth not only for an application of this law of cosmic habit force, but it called for the application of the principle of applied faith. I had to believe that it could be done. I had to think about it and focus on it. The technique that I followed was to give him directions through his subconscious mind.

I did not procrastinate. I did not wait. Every night, for approximately three years, I sat by his crib and directed through his subconscious mind that nature would improvise some form of hearing that would enable him to hear like a normal person. Years later, when he became associated with the great Acousticon Hearing Aid Corporation of the United States, the company doctors, some six or seven of the most outstanding ear specialists in the world, made hundreds of X-rays of Blair's skull, and they said that the psychological treatment which I gave him evidently influenced nature to extend a set of nerves from the center of the brain, or from some portion of the brain, to the inner walls of the skull, enabling him to hear by what they now call bone conduction. At that time, they knew nothing about bone conduction.

In the past thirty-five to forty years, during which I have been working with this philosophy, I have seen the impossible done so many times that I don't recognize that word "impossible" anymore.

I have learned that if you really and truly take possession of your own mind, if you recognize the power of it and learn to make use of the law of cosmic habit force, you can determine your own earthly destiny.

You come into this world without your knowledge or consent, and you go out of it the same way. But while you're here, you have a tremendous scope of operations, during which you can use your mind as you please, constructively or otherwise, for good purposes or bad. It's all up to the individual. You can become a success or you can become a failure, and the way you become a success is by recognizing the power of your mind, by laying out the patterns that you wish to carry out, and by keeping your mind focused on those patterns until this great law of cosmic habit force automatically picks up the patterns and carries them out to their logical conclusion.

It may sound silly to some people to know that I sit on the side of my bed every night and talk to invisible, unseen entities known as the eight guiding princes. It may sound fantastic and impractical. My answer to that, ladies and gentlemen, is that for me it works, and for hundreds of other people to whom I have taught my system, it also works. And that's answer enough.

I don't fool myself in any way about these guiding princes; they are creations of my own mind entirely, as far as I know. But their influence on me is very real. When I make demands upon them, I often get instantaneous returns on those demands.

As many of you know, during these thirty-five or forty years that I have been before the public, I have established a reputation extending throughout two thirds of this civilized world. It has been said by those who have made surveys on the subject that I have helped to make more successful men than any person living at this time. That's quite a claim, and quite a statement. I'm quoting other people. Yet I have reason to believe that statement is true. The reason I have helped to make successful people, ladies and gentlemen, is that I have worked out for myself ways and means of attaining success, and I've reduced my formula to terms which everyone can understand. Just because you may not have heard of some of the formulas that I give you is no reason to doubt that these formulas will work. The thing for you to do is to accept them, to carry them out to the letter. Don't undertake to modify them. Do the things that you are told to do, and do them in the spirit of belief that you're going to get results. If you do, you'll get them.

The next practical application of the great law of cosmic habit force is the development of a system for protecting yourself against outside negative influences. Do you recognize, ladies and gentlemen, that you can't just leave yourself wide open to all of the remarks, to all of the influences, to all of the negative thoughts that are being broadcast through the ether at all times? If I were not immune to negative remarks, I think perhaps I never would have come back to Paris for these radio shows. Because of all the places that I've ever been in my life where people conjured up things to say about me that didn't have any relation to the facts, I've had that experience here. It had no more influence upon me than water upon a duck's back. Not a bit. That is because I recognize that people, in the very nature of things, are suspicious of anything new, and generally suspicious of any new person that comes into the neighborhood. What would have surprised me would have been for me to come into this community and for nobody to have been suspicious of me. I would have thought something was really wrong.

This great law of cosmic habit force means that there are ways and means of giving yourself an immunity against all outside influences, especially the negative ones, the ones that are liable to injure you. If you become true students of this philosophy and learn how to apply it, neither criticism nor other negative remarks will have any influence on you whatsoever. I have never known a person in public life yet who attained any degree of accomplishment who was not criticized. As a matter of fact, there was a very great man who passed this way a long time ago by the name of Christ. When I compare the amount of criticism I get with the amount that he got, I think I'm coming off pretty well.

This system of applying the law of cosmic habit force in giving yourself immunity against the negative things that people believe, and in connection with the thoughts that people broadcast, is one that you can work out very easily. I have it worked out. I call it the three walls of protection. I have around myself one rather high wall and rather wide wall, over which everyone who wishes to communicate with me in any way must jump. When my friend decided to bring me over here to Paris to appear on the radio, he jumped over that wall. He got over it very easily. But immediately he was confronted with another wall, a much higher one, and one not quite so wide. I didn't let him get over that wall quite so easily. Nobody ever gets over that wall unless he has something that I want, something in common with me. That reduces the crowd to a relatively small number. Well, he made the jump, all right, and here I am. But immediately, he was confronted with another high wall, as high as eternity itself, over which neither he nor any other living person ever has or ever will climb. Not even my own wife. That's the place where I go into seclusion and communicate only with infinite intelligence. I communicate through that wall with no one else. At that wall I stop dead every influence that tries to reach my inner consciousness. I simply don't let it go by.

I don't have any voluntary association with anybody who doesn't have some sort of good influence on me. I immediately disassociate myself from the person who carries only negative influences. I don't care who it is. It might even be my mother-in-law or a close relative. Oftentimes, believe you me, I have had to disassociate myself from close relatives.

Next is the use of the law of cosmic habit force in developing a system for the application of faith in your own ability to attain the objects of your earthly destiny as laid out for yourself. You might be surprised to know that ninety-eight percent of the people, even in this great country where we have an abundance of so many things that people need, are not convinced of their ability to get the things they want, right here in the midst of plenty. They suffer from a lack of confidence in self. There is a technique for using the principle of applied faith in the development of that much-needed thing called self-confidence. If I hadn't learned that fact years ago, I never would have had a following of 65 millions of people throughout two thirds of the world. I wouldn't be standing here talking to you tonight. I never would have completed the *Law of Success*—as a matter of fact, I never would have begun it. Because when I was given the assignment by Andrew Carnegie to organize the world's first practical philosophy of individual achievement, it almost scared me to death. I didn't even know the meaning of the word "philosophy." I had to go over to the library and look it up.

But I had an inherent capacity for faith. I began to work on my mind. I began to prepare myself. I began to believe that I could do the thing if Mr. Carnegie said I could do it. And lo and behold, the time came when people stopped laughing, stopped scoffing, and the keenest minds of this world embraced this philosophy, made use of it and recommended it. It has a tremendous following in India because that great personality Mahatma Gandhi came into contact with my success philosophy and ordered it published and distributed throughout India. Of its own accord and on its own merit, it has spread itself throughout more than two thirds of this world.

There's something in that philosophy that came only by my application of faith, by my system of projecting myself and educating myself and preparing myself to do the job. You've got to do the same thing. Life is an eternal proposition of education. You never get through learning. If you really and truly want to make the most of this great prerogative, the privilege which the Creator gave you of using your own mind, you've got to recognize that every day is a day of schooling. It's a schoolhouse, so to speak, a means of educating yourself, of learning more about the ways of nature. You'll never be an educated person, no matter how many degrees you have, unless you understand and adapt yourself to the laws of nature, and especially this great overall comptroller of all of the natural laws known as the law of cosmic habit force.

Next, you should apply the law of cosmic habit force in developing a system for keeping your mind so busy working out ways and means to acquire everything you desire that no time will be left for you to waste in connection with the things you do not desire. Unless I made extensive comment on that particular point, you might overlook it. You may be interested in knowing, ladies and gentlemen, that the majority of people go all the way through this world with their minds fixed upon the fear of poverty, the fear of ill health, the fear of criticism, the fear of the loss of love of someone, the fear of the loss of liberty, the fear of old age, and the fear of death. They have at least those seven fears, and probably a lot more that I haven't time to mention. The major portion of their time is taken up with allowing those fears to discourage them from taking advantage of their own prerogative rights to use their own minds.

What do you suppose those persons are getting out of life? They are getting the things that they allow their minds to dwell upon. That's exactly what they are getting and nothing else. I suspect that there's not a person in this room who hasn't at one time or another suffered with all seven of these basic fears. If you're going to make the most out of the great thing that was given you at birth, the right to control your own mind, you've got to learn that whenever fear appears, there's something in your makeup that needs to be corrected. Fear is something like physical pain; it's an indication that there is a problem that needs to be dealt with.

The most marvelous device of nature is the device of physical pain. It's the one universal language through which nature speaks to every living creature, and which every living creature respects. When you are suffering mental pain through any form of fear, it means there is something in your character, something in your makeup, that you have allowed to get in there that needs to be removed. Those fears are not going to remove themselves, ladies and gentlemen. You've got to remove them. You've got to find the cause; you've got to work out a plan for eliminating that cause, whatever it may be.

Next is the application of the law of cosmic habit force in developing a system for transmuting sex emotion by directing it through creative habits connected with your major purpose in life. I can remember the time when even the very word "sex" couldn't be mentioned in mixed company. Of course, that great emotion is the creative device of nature through which she perpetuates all living species. But I have never found an outstanding person yet, in the pulpit, in law, in medicine, in authorship, in public speaking, in art, or in any other calling, that had not also learned how to convert sexual emotion into doing the constructive things necessary to obtain that person's major objective in life. In the very nature of the subject, I can't go into finer details with an audience like this without risking embarrassment to tender ears, but certainly it is up to you adults to learn the possibilities of making use of the law of cosmic habit force in converting that great creative emotion of nature into the things that you wish to accomplish in this life.

Next is the use of cosmic habit force in a system for developing one or more mastermind alliances from which you may borrow the education, the personality, the specialized knowledge, the experience, and the spiritual forces of others whose cooperation you may need in the attainment of your self-created earthly destiny. Remember, you have here in Paris, Missouri, ladies and gentlemen, a cross section of the American people. You can form mastermind alliances here for the purpose of doing practically anything you wish to carry out, and I hope that you'll each and every one take advantage of that opportunity. What one person can accomplish alone is relatively small. The greater things in life, the bigger and the more worthy undertakings, always have been the result of the coordination in a spirit of friendliness and perfect harmony of two or more minds.

Those of you who are Bible students are quite familiar with the statements that appear in many places in the Bible about the power available when two or more people meet and ask for things in the name of the Master. Those quotations from the Bible have reference to the same thing that I have reference to when I mention the mastermind principle. Because whenever two or more minds come together in a spirit of harmony and are directed to the attainment of a definite objective, there is born of that blending of the minds an outside, invisible power that is available to each one of the individuals. I have never known an outstanding business success or professional success that was not the result of the application of the mastermind.

Next is the application of the law of cosmic habit force in the development of a system which will preclude you from ever speaking of another person in derogatory terms, no matter how much he may deserve it. If you must slander someone, do not speak it, but write it. Write it, though only in the sands near the ocean side, and don't go away until the tides have washed it away. This business of slandering people, and especially slandering people you don't know, like some people in this town have slandered me, is bad. It didn't hurt me. I'm not hurt. I'm not scared. I'm not afraid. I'm not resentful. I feel sorry for them. They haven't learned the great laws of life. They haven't learned that when you criticize another person, you're damaging yourself, whether or not the other person may deserve to be criticized.

You ask me, am I perfect in that? Have I always followed that admonition? I answer you no. Of course I'm not. But I'll tell you one thing: Whenever I have failed to follow that admonition, whenever I have criticized someone, I have always paid for it with some form of sorrow. There's so many good things that you can think and say about people that it hardly behooves you to pick out the worst things that you can think and say about them, as so many people are inclined to do. To avoid that mistake, you must have a system of controlling yourself. Keeping your tongue in your mouth, your mouth closed, and your eyes and ears wide open is a mighty good habit to follow, and let the law of cosmic habit force take that over and carry it out automatically. That would be very helpful to anybody.

Next is the application of the law of cosmic habit force in connection with a daily system of prayer, through which you will express gratitude for all your blessings, naming them one by one. You can choose your blessings in your own wording. Your list of blessings wouldn't be the same as mine, but certainly you have some blessings. You all in the studio have one blessing that I can think of, that I can tell you about right now: You are in pretty good health. You came down here, and you haven't fallen asleep while I'm talking, and you haven't fallen out of your chairs. I haven't seen any of you get mad and go out because I was telling you some of the truths that you might not have been in accord with. So at least you have one thing to be thankful for. You don't have to go very far to find some people who couldn't get down here; they're not able. They're afflicted, or they're afraid. There are people right here in this town who would be afraid to be caught in this crowd. Indeed they would. There are also some who would be afraid not to be caught in it.

Remember, ladies and gentlemen, you can't prosper and have peace of mind without being in tune with the infinite. That's a foregone conclusion. You've got to find ways and means of getting yourself into harmony with that great overall principle known as infinite intelligence. You may call it by some other name, if you choose. But if you did, you and I would still be talking about the same thing.

There are definite ways and means of establishing in your life the kind of habits that you want to see carried out. But you've got to take the initiative. The Creator, while he gave you that great power to use your own mind as you chose, didn't undertake to tell you how to use it. He never will. That's up to you. If you make mistakes, you pay the penalties. If you get on the beam, as we sometimes say, and adapt yourself to these great laws of nature, you get the rewards. Nobody but yourself can keep you away from those rewards.

Next is use of the law of cosmic habit force in the development of a plan by which you will begin teaching the philosophy you have been taught in these lectures, starting with those nearest to you in your own home, in your place of business, or in your neighborhood. Give and you shall receive. No matter what you give, you shall receive in like terms. You'll never have this philosophy mastered any other way. It certainly never will get to you until you start giving it to other people. Just remember that. You don't have to be a great teacher of it, you don't have to be an orator. You only have to be a person who recognizes the soundness of the philosophy and who starts where you stand to pass it on to somebody who may need it. If you look around, I'm sure you will find a lot of people in this community who could profit by this philosophy— especially my broadcast on a positive mental attitude.

Last but not least, let us remember that whatever the mind can conceive and believe, the mind can achieve. I'd like for you to write that down. Put it into letters maybe an inch high, on nice paper. Get an artist to do the job.

Maybe make up three or four of these cards. Put one in the bathroom where you'll see it every day. Put another one in the dining room, where you'll see it every morning when you have breakfast, and put another one in the bedroom, where you sleep at night. Whatever the mind can conceive and believe, the mind can achieve.

How does that happen to be true? It happens to be true because if you conceive a thing and believe it and make a definite picture of it in your own mind, the law of cosmic habit force takes over that picture and guides you to the physical equivalent of that thing, whatever it may be. That's how it happens to be true. You'll be surprised at how many things will come to you that you wanted before, that you worked hard for and didn't get, when you learn how to fasten upon your mind a definite outline of the things that represent to you success in this life.

It is part of nature's plan for rivers to follow the path of least resistance. Crooked rivers create fertile deltas which would not exist if the river ran straight to the sea. All rivers follow the path of least resistance, and it is good that they do. But nature did not intend man to follow such a path. Unfortunately, some men do, to their ultimate regret. Meandering and drifting will not lead to success. One must use the power of cosmic habit force to take the straight and narrow path to success. Failure follows those who do not take this path.

Ladies and gentlemen, you may have noticed that I have referred to rivers often in these broadcasts. Perhaps these references were inspired by the beautiful Salt River, the three forks of which flow into the Mississippi River, and the beautiful Middle Salt which runs right through Paris. It twists and turns lazily, creating rich farmland as well as good fishing and recreation. The people of Paris can enjoy their river, but they must not follow its example. If Paris is to prosper, its people must forge ahead in a straight line, with a purpose and a plan taken over by habit to propel them directly to where they want to go.

Ladies and gentlemen, this concludes my series of broadcasts here in Paris, Missouri, on the principles of success. Members of this community have faced, and continue to face, many adversities. I was invited here by a farsighted businessman in town who has used my teachings to achieve success. He believed my lectures could help you all overcome the obstacles you face. I hope that these broadcasts will help you overcome these adversities and that you will find success and happiness.

Thank you very, very much for welcoming me to Paris. I have greatly enjoyed my time here. Good night and good wishes.